Tea Leaf To Cup

~ From Creation to Modern Cup ~

Clifford Little

ACKNOWLEDGMENTS

I am grateful to the growing number of high quality tea suppliers and, in particular, Don Mei of Mei Leaf for his passion for tea. the inspirational videos on his website and the exceptional teas that Mei Leaf supply.

I acknowledge the many very kind people on Pixabay who have kindly shared their photographs to whom I express my heartfelt gratitude as they put the love of their subject above financial gain as I do with my passion for tea.

I particularly acknowledge the patience of my wife, Judith, who puts up with my tea and teaware filling the cupboards and also for allowing me the time to write this book.

Enjoy Your Tea

CONTENTS

PREFACE

Tea has always been a family drink handed down from generations making tea drinking part of culture throughout the world. Tea is is the world's most popular drink apart from water but in the 70's teabags took over from tea leaves and regrettably the connection with the leaf was lost.

Most British tea drinkers take their tea with milk but as I became older I realised that along with ~40% of the world's population I was intolerant to milk. Interestingly, most Asians including Chinese people are intolerant to milk so do not have milk in their diet. This handicap became a mixed blessing as the real taste of tea became accessible and I became aware that some teas tasted better than others and began experimenting with so called 'speciality teas'.

Starting the journey into tea was like emerging from a black and white world into a full kaleidoscope of colour so, instead of tasting a world of shades of grey, a world of reds, greens, blues, yellows with all the hues and shades imaginable opened up. It was like going through a portal realising that tea was such a diverse product so began trying teas with strange Chinese, Japanese and Indian names and teas which were more expensive. I became fascinated by the history and legends of these teas with unique tastes becoming content to pay some quite hefty prices to obtain teas which expanded my repertoire and knowledge of rare and unusual teas on this never ending journey into the world of tea. There are so many teas available that I will never live long enough to taste those I have on my list as every tea session is a unique experience giving a lifetime of tea tasting.

In my efforts to learn more about tea I searched for books on tea but found very few, so now being a retired Food Scientist I found it necessary to search many different sources. This book is an attempt to explain what this beverage is, where it came from, why it is so widespread and, more importantly, to encourage the reader to move away from the teabag and experiment with high end teas so this is my contribution to show how to navigate through many hundreds of teas on the market by giving some understanding to the way tea flavour is created. I want to encourage the reader to join my journey into tea and connect with the leaf, the legends, the provenance and understand a little of the science and complexity of tea flavour formation. This book is both for those who have already discovered that tea is more than the five or six brands of supermarket black teas looking like pot-pourri, or dust in a paper teabag, and for those who have already discovered the tea world and want to know more about the subject of tea.

I hope the reader enjoys this contribution to tea knowledge as a book which is intended to give an understanding and "taste" of this interesting leaf which has influenced our world.

Image by rawpixel from Pixabay

INTRODUCTION

This book explains the journey of the leaf from creation, discovery by mankind, evolution and cultivation of the plant, manufacture of tea, how each stage of the process has an influence on the tea we drink and how to enjoy the taste of this special leaf. Presenting recent research to explain tea, there is some science explaining tea taste chemicals, a section on how to select, prepare and appreciate tea and an understand of the pricing of tea. This book begins with how tea gained its name, the exact nature of the tea plant and debunks the legend of tea's origins which is reproduced as a fact in almost every tea book and website with more plausible and modern explanations being offered. In short, an attempt has been made to take the tea plant right back to the days of creation, work through how it arrived in the cup and how it can be enjoyed. Tea was once a medicine which evolved into a tonic and is now a worldwide beverage. Tea is a paradox:-

> - **If you are cold tea will warm you, if you are heated tea will cool you**
> - **If you are depressed, tea will cheer you, if you are excited tea will calm you**
> - **If you are tired tea will revive you, if you are awake tea will relax you.**
>
> ## There is always time for tea

Tea creates a relaxed alertness being more than just a drink to quench thirst, it can be a personal, social, sometimes religious experience and to Daoists it has a significance similar to wine's place in Christianity.

Tea is a small leaf, and yet so important to us, has been associated with mankind for millenia influencing social customs throughout the world, changing continents (USA) and empires (Britain) and becoming an important part of some religious practices (Buddhism). It has given the world a pottery industry of porcelain and china clay and contributed to our language and culture, for example, teaspoon, teatime, tea towel, tea dance, tea break and char lady. In the 1960s coffee began to become more popular in Britain and, as with many things from America, gained popularity with the young but never dislodged tea from the number one spot in the world. It is taking time for America to re-appreciate the merits of tea since the unfortunate Boston Tea Party incident took tea off their beverage menu, but tea consumption is now rising in popularity in the USA particularly with good quality speciality teas.

To explain why tea has become so associated with mankind some simple scientific terms have been introduced which may be unfamiliar to some readers but are explained and are fundamental to understanding tea. It is my hope that this contribution will ignite a passion in the reader to learn more about the many teas available.

China, widely recognised as the birthplace of tea, is an exotic society in the east cut off from the Western world by geography. Not only did the continental shift 'build a wall' (the Himalayas) to the South and South West of China but the Chinese themselves built the world's biggest wall to the West and North isolating itself from the rest of the world. (*American Presidents please take note!*). In the 21st century China is becoming more accessible to us in the west since the internet has opened up direct communication making teas with strange and exotic names easily available. Some of these teas can be expensive so guidance is provided on what tea to try and help in where to purchase the teas whilst avoiding some discreditable practises in the market.

> *"China is a sleeping giant. Let her sleep, for when she wakes she will shake the world."*
> *Napoléon Bonaparte (attributed)*
>
> *• ••••••••••*
>
> *The world has nothing to fear from awakening of a*
> *'peaceful lion'*
>
> *Xi Jinping (President of China)*

> *If man has no tea in him, he is incapable of*
> *understanding truth and beauty.*
>
> *Japanese Proverb*

"Tea - the cups that cheer but not inebriate"

William Cowper

In my own hands I hold a bowl of tea; I see all of nature represented in its green color. Closing my eyes, I find green mountains and pure water within my own heart. Silently sitting alone and drinking tea, I feel these become a part of me.

Sen Soshitsu

CHAPTER ONE

TEA – THE NAME

When writing about tea it is important to know exactly what tea really is with one precise word and one precise definition. Whilst this is an obvious statement there is considerable disagreement in academic circles of whether the words used in ancient Chinese text referred to tea or to some other similar bitter plant (they did not have a word for tea) and regrettably, in modern English in the 21st century, this is still the case as the word 'tea' can be as confusing now as when the ancient Chinese wrote about a 'bitter drink'. In those countries that use *cha* there is no confusion there being only one meaning for the word, however, for those countries using *tea* more clarity is required.

Tea In English

The meaning of *tea* in modern usage has come to mean any herbal infusion which includes tea but also includes other herbs such as mint, camomile, nettle, rooibos or the many fruit flavoured herbal infusion which are often based on hibiscus. A word in common usage for these fruit, berry or non-tea herbal infusions is *tisanes*, and the ingredient listing often has hibiscus as a base ingredient with no real tea present. These tisanes, or non-tea infusions, should not be further confused with 'flavoured teas' which are made with real tea flavoured with a fruit or flower such as jasmine, osmanthus or bergamot. The Cambridge Online Dictionary defines 'tisane' as *'a drink made by pouring boiling water onto particular types of dried flowers or leaves'* which leads to some confusion as this definition includes 'real tea' which is a drink made by pouring water onto a dried leaf. The root of the word 'tisane' comes from the Latin word '*ptisana*' meaning crushed, or Greek for peeled barley (pearl barley) or French '*ptisane*' with tisane' being defined in some dictionaries as '*a*

9

medicinal drink originally made from barley soaked in water, (barley water). So the word 'tisane' has evolved over time into its modern usage of 'herbal infusion' and so requires care over this term.

To be clear in this book the word 'tea', as will later be explained, refers to Camellia (C) sinensis as used for commercial tea cultivation. 'Herbal infusions' will not include tea, and the word 'tisane' will refer to non-tea herbal infusions as recognised in modern usage.

Tea In Chinese

Chinese character script is very alien to the Western world which uses an alphabet for the written word, but there is an advantage with Chinese characters in that they are pictorial and universal meaning a particular character conveys the whole word in whatever part of China it is read. When the character is voiced, it would be spoken in whatever dialect the reader speaks thereby overcoming a language barrier in reading. In the west, one European language may be incomprehensible to someone who speaks another European language for example - man (English), homme (French), heren (German) - whereas Chinese script enables Chinese readers to read and understand ancient Chinese writings as easily as reading modern Chinese writing, something which is almost impossible in the west. The disadvantage in Chinese is that it lacks precision so a pictorial character representation of a tea plant in some texts may be referring to a number of different bitter tasting plants. The Chinese initially borrowed the names of other plants for tea one of them being 'Tu', bitter leaf [1], and only the context in which the word 'Tu' is found indicates the more precise meaning which, in this example, could be sow thistle, bitter cabbage, grass, rush or tea. Other borrowed words in Chinese for tea that give confusion to the precise meaning are kia, she, ming (spring sprouts eaten as a vegetable) and chuen (old leaves). The west also has similar problems as 'corn' can mean maize or wheat.

Wang Piu in ~59 B.C in his 'Contract with a Servant' mentions boiling 'tu' purchased from Wutu, a tea district in Schechwan, which scholars believe is a reference to tea but also question the reliability of these ancient documents which were likely to have been written much later. The earliest physical evidence of the beverage was found in the mausoleum of Emporer Jing of Han in Xian and was scientifically proven to be tea as recently as 2016 through chemical analysis of items from the tomb, thus indicating tea was drunk by Han Dynasty emperors as early as the 2nd century B.C. During the Tang dynasty in China, more than ten different words refer to the the meaning of tea, among them, the Chinese character "Tu" was most frequently used but 'tu' can also mean other kind of plants so, from books written in this time, it is not certain if tu is actually a reference to tea, however, some of those references are almost certainly referring to tea.

During the Tang dynasty (A.D. 620-907) the Chinese character "Tu" evolved, by the elimination of a horizontal stroke in the character, to the unique character for tea - "Cha" - which is used today to specifically mean tea. Anything written before this time using the current Chinese character for tea is considered to be rewritten at a later date from the original. Lu Yu, a Chinese Scholar, wrote the first book about tea around 760A.D. called the "Cha Ching" (Classic of Tea), now considered a major literary masterpiece from the Tang dynasty, and used the unique character for 'cha' although we know tea was being consumed well before this date both as a vegetable and as a beverage. Some sources believe that the character first made its appearance in the 'Erh Ya' a Chinese dictionary, as revised by Kuo Po, around 350 A.D. when tea was being cultivated.

Left: Cha with one horizontal stroke. Right a second horizontal stroke at the top of the vertical stroke, meant any 'bitter tasting leaf'.

Lu Yu used this character for 'cha' comprising three radicals to denote tea placing man between the tree and the grass radical. This now remains the Chinese character for the subject of this book. The similarity between the old and new characters suggests a common origin.

When the Chinese traded tea the word used was cha or cha-ye (tealeaf) so many countries now refer to tea as *cha* or derivatives of the word - Cha (Japan), chay (Turkey), chai (Russia), shai (Arabic). Notably, the only European country to call the beverage 'cha' is Portugal with other European countries, America and some other countries referring to our subject as 'tea' and derivatives of the word tea – Té (France), Thee (Dutch), Tey (Tamil), Teja (Latvia). So from where does the word 'tea' come from?

Portugal was the first European country to trade with China, encountering tea in 1560 and were granted a trading port at Macau, now a special administrative region south of Guangdong (Canton) province where Cantonese is spoken. The locals were found to be very fond of making an infusion of a strange herb in hot water which, due to its popularity, the Portuguese took home. - this herb was called 'cha' in the local dialect of Cantonese spoken around the ports of Macau. The main Chinese languages, Mandarin and Cantonese, use *cha* as the word for tea. The next Europeans to arrive in China were the Dutch who could not trade or land at Macau as neither the Portuguese nor the Chinese would allow that, but they were granted a trading port further north at Amoy, now Xiamen, in Fujian province. In this seaport, along the Southern coast of China, the Min Chinese Hokkien dialect word 'te', pronounced 'tay', is used. The Dutch became the primary traders between Europe and Asia, indeed the main export harbour for Europe bacame Amoy with the ports at Macau, near Hong Kong becoming less used in those days. In the words of the great tea adventure Robert Fortune in his book published 1847 "Three Years Wandering in the Northern provinces of

China" page 18, "*Viewed as a place of trade, I fear Hong Kong will be a failure*", (a little wrong there Robert!). The European countries that Holland traded with adopted the local word '*tay*' so the two words, tay and cha, made their separate ways into other languages around the world – inland routed tea *cha* became the word for tea, seaward routed tea the word '*tay*' was used with Portugal remaining the only European country to use the word 'cha'. It was first spelt 'tea' in 1660 but continued to be pronounced 'tay' rhyming with 'obey' -

> *Here thou great Anna whom three realms obey,*
> *Dost sometimes counsel take – and sometimes tea.*
> *Rape of the Lock, Pope (1711)*

- until sometime between 1720 and 1748 when the pronunciation in English changed to tea[23]

> *"One day in July last at tea,*
> *And in the house of Mrs. P."*
> *The Trial of Sarah Palmer, John Gay's play, Edward Moore.*
> *(~1748)*

The reason is not known but the Irish word for tea is 'tae' but the diphthong 'æ' is pronounced 'ee' so somewhere between local accents, spelling and pronunciation the word changed to tea (tee).

CHAPTER TWO

TEA PLANT TAXONOMY

Tea, for the English in the 19th century, bacame an extremely important commercial product and China had a monopoly on the prodct for both cultivation and manufacture which was clearly not ideal for such an important commercial product particularly as trade in China was problematical. To secure a source of this valuable commodity it was necessary to understand the taxonomy of the tea plant so that the correct plant could be grown outside China. The exact taxonomy of the tea plant is complicated mainly in identifying where to place any tea plant varient into an exact genus, species, variety, and sub-variety which have been created by exchanges of genetic material occurring relatively freely within plant members of the tea genus. The tea plant group has many overlapping traits and hardly any vegetative feature that show such a discontinuous variation so is difficult to separate into discrete taxonomic groups.

The plant was first classified by the Swedish botanist, physician, and zoologist Carl Linnaeus, the "father of modern taxonomy', who formalised the modern system of naming organisms in the work 'Species Plantarum', published in 1753, which was the starting point of modern botanical nomenclature. The first volume was issued on 24th May, the second volume 16th August of the same year containing 1,200 pages describing over 7,300 species. The tea plant was first listed as 'Thea sinensis' but later in the same work it was listed as 'Camellia', which later botanists believed to be the same genus as Thea, and argued until very recently whether the tea plant should be Camellia or Thea i.e. the same or seperate genera. Linnaeus recognized two species of tea based largely on black tea - 'Thea (T) bohea' (pronounced "boo-hee") - and green tea - Thea viridis' - so withdrew T. sinensis leaving Camellia. The name Bohea was named after the Wuyi mountains, from where black tea was first traded with

Europe, and being so different from green tea it was regarded as a seperate plant from the green tea plant. (It was quite normal in the 18th century to order a cup of bohea meaning tea). It was a later botanist, J.Sims in 1807 who joined bohea and viridis back to the name 'Thea sinensis' and Robert Fortune, the horticulturist employed by the East India Company, who went to China to collect tea seeds, who confirmed in his book "Three Years Wandering the Provinces of China" published 1847 page 187, that bohea and viridis were from the same plant and that it was only the manufacturing process that made green tea turn black, so the species name was agreed to be Thea (Camellia) 'sinensis'.

Matters became more complicated when, in 1823, the British discovered tea growing in India, although the indiginous Indians had always known about this plant, but if the Indian plant was accepted as tea the taxonomy question was where this tea fitted in as it was different to the China plant. Curiously, in 1825 Indian tea leaves and seeds were sent to Dr. Nathaniel Wallich of the Botanical Gardens in Calcutta who insisted that the plant he received was not tea but a Camellia! It was not until 1834 that the Indian tea plant in Assam was confirmed as being tea but a seperate *variety* of the plant and this, 'coincidentally', was also the first year of trading in China after the East India Company had lost the monopoly of trading in China which meant the company really needed another source of this valuable commodity. However, was this new tea a seperate *species* - Thea assamica, or *variety* - Thea sinensis assamica? Botanists tried new names for the conjoined teas such as Seamann in 1859 '*Thea chinensis*' meaning any species of tea, and Cohen-Stuart (1919) calling this species *Camellia theifera.* However, many other botanists recognised the Assam plant as a variety of the sinensis species leaving the names chinensis, theifera, bohea and viridis synonyms of the same species so redundant terms. While the nomenclature of the tea plant was agreed to be Camellia (genus), the position of the two taxa, represented by the sinensis and the assam plants, still remained

15

open to question - where to place the Assam plant - as a seperate species, Camellia assamica, or new variety of the sinensis species, Camellia sinensis assamica. The current weight of evidence is that the Assam and China tea plants differ at the level of variety. The International Botanical Congress in 1935 decided Camellia sinensis (L) to be the correct name of tea plant species so two distinct taxa of commercial tea are now recognised -

- Camellia (genus) sinensis (species) sinensis (variety) being the small-leaved China plant -
- Camellia (genus) sinensis (species) assamica (variety)the large-leaved Assam plant .

As an aside, *Camellia japonica (Japan)* contains the ornamental garden flower group and *Camellia sinensis (China)* is the tea plant *group*. To be clear, 'Thea', as the genus name, is no longer appropriate but is sometimes used to group Camellia plants which make a form of tea, even though some of these teas are not used commercially, in the same way that a grouping may be the 'ornamental' group.

Regularly mentioned as a third variety of tea is the 'Java bush' C. *cambodiensis (lasiocalyx)* which has been used to crossbreed with other tea varieties to achieve certain traits in other tea cultivars but the Java bush is not used in commercial tea production. The issue is whether lasiocalyx is a variety – *Camellia sinensis lasiocalyx* or a sub-variety of assamica - *Camellia sinensis assamica subvariety lasiocalyx*. The most recent opinion is that it is a hybrid of the large leaf Chinese Assam tea found in Yunnan, and the Indian Assam tea type tea and is therefore a subspecies of Camellia sinensis assamica[16].

The problem botanists encounter with tea is that the Camellia plant split into different taxa then interbred between these new species and varieties and each new hybrid continued to evolve and interbreed such that tea is regarded as a good example demonstrating gene plasticity where there is hardly any plant which is truly pure. It is probably best to leave the botanical assignment to botanists to argue over and treat it as a subvariety of assam tea that is not a commercial tea and go for a cuppa!

In addition to commercial teas, wild grown non-commercial tea species are sometimes locally used to prepare tea beverages instead of cultivated C. sinensis due to accessibility and include C. taliensis, C. grandibractiata, C. kwangsiensis, C. gymnogyna, C. crassicolumna, C. tachangensis, C. ptilophylla and C. irrawadiensis[2]. Some of these species do not contain caffeine, such as irrawadiensis and ptilophylla, so are not classified as true commercial tea but special mention is made of C. taliensis as this plant is a close ancient relative of modern tea similar to the large leafed Yunnan assam variety and is sometimes used to make traditional Yunnan Puerh tea. A great deal of research is being carried out on this species as it is an ancient variety that may be used as a a gene bank in modern monocultured plantations and being a close relative of C. sinensis it can easily be crossed with C. assamica which it resembles.

Commercial tea taxonomy is now considered as :-

- Kingdom Plantae – Plants
    - Subkingdom Tracheobionta – Vascular plants
        - Superdivision Spermatophyta – Seed plants
            - Division Magnoliophyta – Flowering plants
                - Class Magnoliopsida – Dicotyledons
                - Subclass Dilleniidae
                    - Order Theales
                    - Family Theaceae – Tea family Genus Camellia L.

- Species Camellia sinensis (L.) Kuntze

- **Variety Camellia sinensis (L.) Kuntze var. sinensis**

- **Variety Camellia sinensis (L.) Kuntze var. assamica (J. Masters) Kitam.**

Commercial tea is from the following list and any subvariety or clonal variety:-

- Camellia sinensis var. sinensis (small-leaf China bush)

- Camellia sinensis var. assamica (large-leaf India bush)

- Wild-growing and ancient tea trees naturally growing in southwest China, Laos, Myanmar, northern Thailand and northern Vietnam

Camellia sinensis - Image by Natasha G from Pixabay

CHAPTER THREE

TEA PLANT ORIGINS

It is natural with anything of significance to mankind that there is a desire to trace the history back as far as possible to the beginning and three issues exercise mankind in the pursuit of the beginning of tea: Firstly, where and when did the plant originate; secondly, when did mankind first consume tea; thirdly, where and when was tea first cultivated. Tea history goes back so far in time that most of the sources predate the written word, so archaeology and legend play a significant part and more recently genetic traceability is beginning to shed light on tea's origins. The tea plant is 'Camellia sinensis' with two main tea varieties - variety sinensis and variety assamica.

The Legendary Origin of Man Meeting Tea

The mysterious Orient is well known for myths and legends and one legend appears in almost every book and website on tea history so, for completeness, the myth variations are related below. As a word of caution, the legend does not need to be true to have truth in it as these legends explain man meeting tea. They involve the legendary Emperor of China, Shen Nong, also known as the Wugushen or Divine Emperor, who is credited with inventing agriculture and Chinese medicine and is mentioned in 'The Classic of Tea' by Lu Yu, the first book about tea written in the 8th centuryA.D. The tea legend variations are shown below and the veracity of them discussed afterwards.

(a)   Some time around 2737 BC Shen Nong was drinking a bowl of boiled water when a few leaves were blown from a nearby tree into the bowl. He tasted the resulting liquor, and the beverage tea was born.

(b)   The Emperor Shen Nong, god of agriculture, tested the medical properties of various herbs on himself and, reputedly having a transparent stomach, the effects of the herbs could be clearly seen so he could tell whether plants had beneficial or poisonous effects but if things went wrong he found tea to work as an antidote. Shen Nong found this later, to his cost, to be erroneous and died from a toxic overdose of a herb when he ate the yellow flower of a weed which caused his intestines to rupture before he had time to swallow his tea antidote. **The message is clear - Do not try this at home it does not work!**

(c)   Shen Non Shi (Shennong clan) when out with his family became thirsty when a leaf drifted onto his foot. He picked up the leaf , twisted the leaf with his fingers and the juice on his fingers tasted bitter. He believed that this leaf could have medicinal properties and could quench thirst when infused.

The essence of these legends is that Shen Nong discovered tea accidentally, by some divine intervention, or tested tea on himself as he did with other herbs. In both cases he found the plant appealing in taste and it also had restorative properties.

Shen Nong, which can be translated as "God Farmer ", "God Peasant" or "Agriculture God", was one of three sovereigns, or deified kings in China and he is given credit for various agricultural inventions including the hoe, cart, plough, axe, digging wells, agricultural irrigation, preserving stored seeds by using boiled horse urine, weekly farmers' market, taming the ox, and yoking the horse so reputedly established a stable agricultural society in China. His medical status is due to having refined the therapeutic understanding of taking pulse measurements, acupuncture, moxibustion and instituting the harvest thanksgiving ceremony. He spoke after three days of his birth, walked within a week, started ploughing the field when he was three years old, cleared the land with fire and established the Chinese calender. The Ben Cao Jing (Pen Tsao) "The Classic of Herbal Medicine", an agricultural and medical book of herbs and their uses, is attributed to him although not written down until the third century A.D. but he is respected as the father of Chinese medicine. If he did just a little of what legend attributes to him he must have been quite a character!

Wikipedia Image. Shennong as depicted in a 1503 painting by Guo XuShen Nong was thought to be ox-headed, sharp-horned, bronze-foreheaded, and iron-skulled.

The question remains is whether these apocryphal legends have any grain of truth in them as there are no written Chinese records prior to 1300 B.C. Ascribing the discovery of tea to a revered former leader is a characteristically Confucian gesture putting power in the hands of the ancestors and links the present day to the mythical past. Shen Nong history relies on archaeological evidence, of which there is none, not even for the Xia dynasty which came later and is the legendary, possibly apocryphal, first dynasty in traditional Chinese history. It is more likely that Shen Nong Shi was the name of a primitive farming tribe rather than one individual and possibly tea played an important role in this clan. The indication of his actual existence lies in the term '*Mythical Emperor*'.

We must consider that Shen Nong did not *write* the Ben Cao Jing (Pen Tsao) as there was no written medium in 28th century B.C. It was more likely a compilation of oral traditions put into a written form in the Neo-Han dynasty A.D 25-221, three thousand years after Shen Nong's existence, with the reference to tea being added a further 500 years later in the 7th century A.D. when the word 'cha' came into use. This is an astonishing 3400 years after Shen Nong and is at a time when we have little idea of this ancient world now nearly 5 millennia in the past. There is no evidence that Shen Nong ever really existed and it is absurd that mere accident of wind blowing a leaf into the cup of an experimental herbalist ever occurred. The Ben Cao being unwritten for over 3000 years and the date 2737 A.D. being so specific make the plausibility of this legend very low even for the low threshold of probability that legends usually have. Clearly, all the great discoveries attributed to him are highly unlikely to have been one person or even one tribe.

This persistent legend is so widespread, being reproduced in almost every book without qualification,,and presented and accepted as fact. Nevertheless, Shen Nong is still worshipped on his birthday on April 26th, at temples dedicated to him. So there you have it, a *mythical* emperor with no evidence of either his, or his successor's, existence has not only a precise year of being emperor but a specific date of birth.

Evolution of Tea [3]

Evolutionary evidence to find the origin of the tea plant is also helpful by going back into the days of Earth's formation and working forward to the origins of the modern tea plant which evolved from its Camellia ancestors, as this will give background to the history of the tea plant.

The largest landmass as Earth developed was called Gondwana[3] which

22

spread from the equator to the South Pole with smaller scattered land masses throughout the rest of the globe. As plants evolved on land, the continental plates would have moved to form one large landmass called Pangea, spread roughly equally over the two hemispheres and then slowly drifted apart into the continents as we now know them, this process still ongoing today, with global temperatures fluctuating between warm periods and ice ages. Land plant evolution occurred, and still continues, with species being trapped in their continents following different evolutionary paths on whichever landmass they happened to be.

The continental drift continued with the Atlantic Ocean opening up and separating America from Europe and the Grand Canyon opening up. Meanwhile the Indian and Eurasian tectonic plates were colliding around 50 million years ago causing a crumpling effect on the Earth's crust and raising the Himalayas with some landmass extrusion to the South and East. The Himalayas are still rising, albeit very slowly, at about half a centimetre per year, making Mount Everest higher now than when Sir Edmund Hillary stood on the summit. Most of this process occurred in the last 10 million years being the period when Camellia sinensis evolved. The significance of the Himalayas is that they have a marked influence on the climate in Eastern and Southern Asia and act as a barrier to people migration, communication and the spread of plants which usually spread east and west keeping to a defined geographical latitude. In Yunnan, China, the mountain ranges formed run in north-south ridges with differing altitudes so plants were not trapped within a narrow range of latitude and could spread more easily north and south. Additionally the Himalayas create the monsoon rainfall and Camellia sinensis requires annual rainfall of at least 120 cms per year which is found in south west Yunnan a region in south west China which has an ancient history based on tea culture. Once the ancient tea plants had evolved they needed to continue to evolve to survive life's threats.

One aspect of evolution relevant to tea is the fact that plants invaded the land from the sea and and being unable move became vulnerable to lack of water and herbivores that eat plants which have captured and stored energy from the sun. Predators, such as animals and insects, would have flourished depleting plant life until equilibrium between plants and herbivores was reached. Evolutionary pressure caused plants to adopt defence mechanisms against these predators, e.g. physical defences such as spines, hairs or woody tissue, then improved these defences when *angiosperms* (plants rather than ferns which are *gymnosperms*) evolved a characteristic sac inside the plant cell called a *vacuole.* This is like a storage kit bag where defence *secondary metabolite* chemicals are stored to help the plant defend itself. - *Primary metabolites* are chemicals essential for an organisms normal life, growth, development and reproduction - *secondary metabolites* are not necessary to sustain life but are of value to the plant but may interfere with the cell biochemistry if they were present in the main plant cell cytoplasm. These stored secondary metabolites can be used when required to help the plant survive acting as repellants or attractants. For example they may give the plant a repellent taste or smell to deter insect herbivores or an odour to attract the herbivores predators. A co-evolutionary explosion was created where plants developed improved defence mechanisms causing insects to evolve ways round these defences for their own survival and this in turn led to plants evolving more complex defences, and this evolutionary proceess continues to this day. It is precisely these defensive chemicals which provide much of the flavour of tea.

Genetic Origins

In 1978, 35.4 million year old fossils of broad leaf *magnolia latifolia* and *magnolia miocenia* from the Theaceae family believed to be related to large leaf tea were discovered in Manxian, Jinggu, Lancang, Jingdong and Tengchong in

24

southwestern Yunnan[17] indicating a possible location of the original tea plants. The seeds of Camellia are large so do not travel easily without a vector so Camellias initially spread slowly outside this Indo-China region before artificial propagation by man. This slow geographical movement, due to low seed dispersal, makes genetic traceability possible as neighbouring trees share common genetic traits. Truly wild, original trees are now considered non-existent and any extant ancient tea trees (Camellia sinensis or related species) are more likely to be feral trees gone wild from earlier cultivation rather than truly forest 'wild trees', nevertheless many old trees of ages possibly beyond 1000 years old have been found in Yunnan province in China and the Assam district of India. What was needed to locate a more precise origin was traceability between wild trees and modern domesticated, cultivated trees, called *tea trees in transition*. It is generally accepted that Indo-China was the birthplace of tea but national pride divided into whether tea originated in north west India or south east China.

In Yunnan, some tea trees are very different to most of the cultivated tea trees grown in the rest of China being closer to the Indian assamica variety than the sinensis variety and are known as 'Yunnan Large Leaf' (Da Ye). Also in this region are other wild camellias including one closely related species called *Camellia taliensis,* or 'Wild Tea variety' (wild - because it is not cultivated) so this area, in the lower reaches of the Lancang (Mekong) river, became a likely place for seeking trees in transition to a domesticated tea plant. The region is well known for a special fermented broad leaf tea called Puerh tea which is named after the city once known as Simao in Yunnan and is made from Yunnan Large Leaf which may be a wild tree, a cultivated tree turned wild, a cultivated tree or sometimes from the related ancient species Camellia taliensis. Genetic divergence has indicated that C. taliensis var. bangwei is a semi-wild transient landrace occupying a genetic position between wild and cultivated tea plants –

tea tree in transition! The spread of Camellia is now being extensively studied by DNA analysis as it is possible to trace local landraces through neighbouring trees. It is this genetic fingerprint that makes research into varieties like Camellia taliensis so important as these ancient varieties of tea plant contain genes lost in modern cultivars but may prove useful in defending against future threats to the monocultured tea plants by insects and plant diseases.

A link now exists between small leaf tea in eastern China, large leaf tea in Western China and prehistoric tea fossils. Evidence was needed to show that these wild trees became cultivated through the 'tea trees in transition' which was sought in the Yunnan area around Mount Tingmai called 'Six Tea Hills' where there are many ancient trees reputedly ~1000 years old. Many ancient wild trees have been discovered growing in Jiujia Township, 200 kilometres from Jinggu, and also in Bangwai village (Yunnan) where scattered, uncultivated tea trees were found different to the usual Chinese domesticated trees in that the reproductive parts, flowers and fruit, are similar to wild trees whilst the vegetative parts, leaves and branches, are similar to cultivated trees. These trees were considered to have an evolutionary link between wild and cultivated trees and possibly tea trees in transition. A study in 1981 reported tea plants, leaves, flowers and seed also showed marked differences from each other in the Dalau mountain range which ajoins Sichuan, Guizhou and Yunnan which were not affected by the glacial age, many ancient plants survived there, and this allegedly put the birthplace of tea in the plateau of Yunnan - so southern Sichuan, western Yunnan and northern Guizhou is considered the birthplace of tea, although, in reality, we can never know for sure the precise location of the first tea plants. Nevertheless, analysis of the chromosomes on wild tea showing tea tree in transition characteristics led to Huang Guiqiu, a leading figure in the puerh tea industry to state rather simplistically in at a conference at the International Symposium on Chinese Puerh Tea April 1993, that the dispute over the origins of tea between India and China was finally settled - *'China is the home of tea; Yunnan is the world origin of the tea tree. Yunnan, southern Sichuan to western Hunan and northern Guizhou. district and both sides of the Lancang (Mekong) River are the concentrated regions of the source of the tea tree'*. However, it must be said, that this is by no means fully confirmed and remains an opinion only but is very likely as indicated by more recent, genetic studies.

Yunnan   Sichuan   Guizhou

Provinces in China - Wikipedia

The question still remained whether tea actually came from two separate sources, assamica (Indian) and sinensis (Chinese), or whether one evolved from the other. The tea community once believed that assamica evolved into sinensis as the plant spread to colder, higher regions and that the assamica plant was a retrograde, unrefined tea plant. The latest hypothesis that assam and sinensis varieties diverged naturally, and later Indian Assam diverged from one or both of these ancestors as tea began to be domesticated seems supported by evidence. Genetic research indicates that the differences in tea plants are likely to be the result of *three* independent domestication events from three separate regions across China and India - the China sinensis type tea, Chinese Assam type tea and Indian Assam type tea[16]. Evidence suggests that C. assamica and C. sinensis diverged naturally, ~22,000 years ago (T1) coinciding with the last glacial maximum and subsequently the third linneage, Indian Assam, evolved ~2770 years ago (T2) largely by domestic cultivation, coinciding with the legendary beginnings of tea. (*Come back Shen Nong – all is forgiven!*). The

Yunnan-Guizhou Plateau is the area of differentiation for commercial Camellia tea varieties. North of 25° latitude in the Yunnan-Guizhou Plateau C. sinensis var. sinensis predominates whilst in the south it is C. sinensis var. assamica. The small-leaf variety is dominant in eastern China, Taiwan and Japan and the broad-leaf dominates in India.. They can and have all interbred with each other, and also with wild varieties such as taliensis probably during domestication, causing a massive overlapping of genes and almost a genetic continuum with little definite seperation between varieties. Crop domestication is dynamic giving rise to landraces which are the basis of modern tea cultivars.

In southern Yunnan (Puerh area) C. assam type tea contains C. taliensis genetic material and is distinct from western Yunnan C. assamica (Lincang area) where the genetic material is similar to Indian C. assamica. Hybridization occurs where these varieties overlap as all the varieties can interbreed which confuses the issue. Meegahakumbura et al[16] concluded that western Yunnan Assam tea and Indian Assam tea both may have originated from the same parent plant in the area where southwestern China, Indo-Burma, and Tibet meet. However, as the Indian Assam tea shares no specific genetic markers (haplotypes) with western Yunnan (Chinese) Assam tea (it is significantly genetically different), Indian Assam tea is likely to have originated from an independent domestication and model C is the most likely tea evolutionary path. The parentage of modern tea plants follows the hypothetical model below with all three linneages existing and interbreeding in the Yunnan area.:-

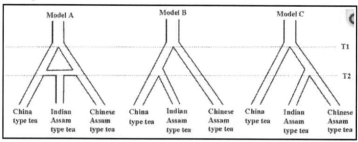

Three demographic history models tested for tea domestication[4]

28

Cultivation origins

In the Puerh region in Yunnan live a colourful ethnic tribe known as the Bulang whose culture is very closely associated with tea, as their leader Pa Aileng made the whole tribe drink tea to cure a sickness which almost wiped out this small tribe thus making tea central to their culture. Just before he died he wrote:-

> *I cannot leave you horses and cows, they would die from disasters; I cannot leave you money and treasure, because you will use them up. I leave you the tea trees, so your descendants will never use them up.*

Zhuge Liang, a military leader in this area, also known as Zhu Ge Liang or Kongming (A.D. 181–234), encouraged the Yunnan people to cultivate tea due to its sustaining properties in battle and is considered the first to cultivate tea in this area becoming known as 'The Father of Tea' with Puerh city containing a large commemorative statue of him. Tea is so engrained in the culture that sacrifices to this tea god and their ancestors are offered every year in April and they refer to the tea tree as the Kongming tree. He is often depicted wearing a Taoist robe holding a hand fan made of crane feathers, named a 'Kongming fan' after him.

Zhuge Liang courtesy of Konegan, Flikr.com

Tea cultivation is believed to have started in this general region and began to spread from Yunnan, eastwards towards the coast over a long period of time and, in the process of domestication, tea evolved by agricultural selection. An analogy would be a crab apple turning into a modern Cox's Orange Pippin or Golden Delicious apple through centuries of plant selective breeding. Domestication must have occurred long before this, probably about 3,000 years ago so is one of the earliest tree crops in China. Excavations of the Hang Yangling Mausoleum in Xian, Shaanxi province, China, revealed tea drinking by Liu Qi, Emperor Jing of Han dynasty, at least 2,100 years ago indicating it was in their culture and so domesticated. It is clear that there are multiple centers of tea cultivation so the 'first' will never be absolutely confirmed as the following archeological finds show.

Neolithic Tea[5.21]

In 2001 a Neolithic settlement of the Hemudu tribe that existed 6000-3500B.C. was discovered near the Eastern coast of China at the foot of Tianluoshan (Snail Hill) near the city of Ningbo in Zhejiang province eastern China. The Hemudu people were an agrarian society that cultivated and stored many crops so cultivation of any plant was possible. Nearby, in early 2004, 7 kilometres from Mount Siming, a dozen rhizomes were found in good preservation in pits one metre below ground in a ten square metre regular pattern of rows. The pits were filled with loose, light coloured soil which contrasted with the surrounding dark, compacted soil suggesting that the rhizomes may have been deliberately planted. Fortunately the roots were well preserved as the site in Neolithic times was surrounded by marshland with the area regularly flooding shifting the river systems and sea so, when the site was abandoned, sediment covered the area sealing the pits in an anaerobic condition. These rhizomes were believed to be Camellia, and the plant structures indicated they may be tea. The roots required further analysis but every indication was that they belonged to the plant family group Theaceae, genus Camellia, so they were stored in the Hemudu Site Museum for later analysis. The exact nature of the roots had not been positively identified nevertheless, discovery of Neolithic tea was announced in September 2004 at the Eighth International Tea Culture Symposium at Yanan, Sichuan. In 2008 the Zhejiang Bureau of Cultural Relics arrranged for the roots to be tested and the amino acid theanine was found which is almost exclusive to Camellia Sinensis. In the tea plant (Camellia Sinensis) theanine is formed in the roots and transferred to the leaves and is a useful chemical marker to identify tea. Carbon dating put the age of the roots at 3,526-3,366 B.C. with an 87.7 percent possibility. In other words, cultivation of tea may have begun in the lower Yangtze region over 5400 years ago.

The significance of this find, if verified, cannot be underestimated as the tea plant appears to be cultivated predating the Shen Nong legend with a much wider geographical spread than previously believed being in eastern China. It is postulated that the tea plant, Camellia sinensis, originated in western China and spread along the Yangtze river becoming more cultivated until it arrived at the Eastern seaports, so finding cultivated tea on the Eastern sea is something quite new. Extrapolating backward leads to the hypothesis that tea plant usage originated nearer the beginning of the Hemudu tribe's existence (6000B.C.) and cultivation between 3,500 and 6,000BC.

So, are we any further forward in determining the origins of cultivated tea? Not yet, as the bar for scientific certainty is very high. In legal type terms, a legend needs a few percentage points of plausibility for it to be based on any reality, scientific theories need a 'balance of probabilities' or 50+% to have credibility, and to be scientific fact it must be 'beyond any reasonable doubt' or 98+%. This latest discovery is currently at the 'balance of probabilities' stage.

There is ongoing discussion[7] about whether the tea plant found was actually cultivated as there is agreement that the roots found are Camellia but not whether they were actually planted. It could be that the different coloured soil on the roots was naturally formed along the growth of the expanding roots and the plant row spacing may well be coincidental. Tianluoshan is five metres above sea level but marshy ground is not a good place to cultivate Camellia so the connection between the settlement and the plants remains unclear. Further to this, whilst all agree that the plant is Camellia, there is no agreement to the species and there is no confirmed, truly wild Camellia sinensis with which to compare the plants. This does not rule out cultivation of tea and the general concensus is that the rhizomes are Camellia sinensis, deliberate planting is possible but not certain and further work is needed as solid proof is lacking.

In January 2019 a renowned Indian tea researcher and explorer, Pradip Baruah,, reported on a visit to the Old Doidam area north of Myanmar in southeastern Arunachal Pradesh, India's fifth largest tea producing state, that he found many wild, ancient tea trees and met with members of the Noktey tribe who demonstrated how they make Khelap, the native word for tea. Tribal people still rely on tea's medicinal properties, an awareness that dates to Neolithic times (*allegedly*) but there is no knowledge or evidence of any cultivation.

Pre-Homo Sapiens Origin

According to Mair and Hoh (The True History of Tea, 2009, p.27) Homo sapiens most likely encountered the tea plant in the migration out of Africa to Asia approximately 55,000 years ago, much older than previously discussed. One method of harvesting tea leaves is to seek out wild trees and pluck the leaves which often entails climbing the trees to pick them so some trees are chopped down to access the leaves which is a technique elephants use in Africa, but in so doing the source of the leaves is permanently destroyed so ancient tea trees in Yunnan now have protected status. As tea became more popular there became a need to to secure a regular source so tea trees began to be cultivated by man and then varieties improved with increasing selective domestication.

Plants are the primary source of energy capture from the sun for all living organisms as all land animals are evolved from animals that derive their food from plants. Animals would have naturally evolved an awareness of which plants were especially beneficial, which were not and which plants harmed them. Some plants are beneficial, not because of the food value, but because of the medicinal properties and it is not just humans that have this knowledge, it is an inbuilt animal trait. Tea is a mildly bitter, astringent plant containing chemicals which have an effect on the consumer and one of the main chemicals is caffeine, a mild stimulant which improves mental and physical performance. Tea, apart from being a beverage is still consumed for health reasons.

Image by Pete Linforth from Pixabay

University of Georgia ecologist Ria R. Ghai[6] and her colleagues observed a troop of more than 100 colobus monkeys in Uganda's Kibale National Park for four years and noted that monkeys infected with a whipworm parasite were

33

found to spend more time resting and less time moving, grooming and having sex. The infected monkeys ate twice as much tree bark as their healthy counterparts even though they kept the same feeding schedules.The bark sweeps the intestinal intruder out of the simians' gastrointestinal tracts and additionally seven of the nine species of trees and shrubs preferred by sick monkeys have known pharmacological properties, such as antisepsis and analgesia, indicating the monkeys may have been self-medicating. This behaviour is known as *zoopharmacognosy*, in which non-human animals self medicate typically involving ingestion or topical application of plants, soils or insects in order to prevent or reduce the harmful effects of pathogens and toxins. The monkeys and local people were using the same plants to treat illnesses including infection by whipworm parasites. Elephants have also been observed eating charcoal from forest fires believed to be taken as an aid to digestion. Four individual wild orangutans were seen rubbing a soothing naturally occurring anti-inflammatory balm onto their limbs and local people use the same balm administered in a similar manner to treat aches and pains, so early examples of orangutans self medicating. Another well-known example of zoopharmacognosy occurs when dogs eat grass to induce vomiting.

Mankind consumes three main beverages, tea, coffee and cacao (cocoa) which all contain caffeine which acts as a tonic, so it may be that tea consumption of leaves, then infusion, started before mankind evolved into home sapiens thus making tea older than humans today.

Summary of tea origins

The legend of Shen Nong is colourful and widespread but he is a mythical person whose existence has no proof other than oral tradition and dating this mythical person with 2737B.C. stretches credibility too far. The legend serves as an easy, some would say too simplistic, way to explain a complex subject of an ancient, complex plant. Genetic evidence is more reliable in how the plant came into existence, both by natural evolution and by domesticated breeding, but the most probable geographical origin is believed to be South Western China, North West India, Myanmar (Burma) with an evolutionary cultivated path eastwards towards the coast with sinensis and two seperate domesticated paths of assamica, one in Yunnan and one in India with strong genetic evidence pointing to this conclusion. The unproven archaeological findings at Tianluoshan throw some confusion to dating the connection between tea and mankind mainly due to the distance from Western China and this continues to be investigated.

One view is that tea predates homo sapiens and was always a plant known to pre-human animals in the area where it originated in the Yunnan-Guizhou Plateau in south western China. Humans evolved knowing that Camellia sinensis was an effective medication or tonic and the path of tea from medicine to tonic to beverage began before present mankind existed. This may be so but the cultivation of tea probably dates back to around 200A.D. to the Bulang tribe in Yunnan or possibly earlier in other tribes in the Yunnan area.

Tea plant seeds are large and do not travel easily so interbreeding between bushes in close proximity to each other leads to gene clusters, and cultivation leads to reduced genetic variation so these properties are used to determine how the plant spread. This has led to our present understanding of tea's origins:-

Ancesters of modern domesticated tea, originated somewhere in the Indo-China region of northern India, southwest China, Laos, Myanmar, up to 35 million years ago - Tea was consumed by mankind possibly as far back as homo sapiens existed - Tea was **cultivated** around 3000 years ago with three lines of ancesters, C. sinensis, C. assamica (Indian type) and C. assamica (Chinese type).

CHAPTER FOUR

TEA CULTIVATION

Varieties, Sub-Varieties, Landraces and Cultivars

It is now believed that the tea plant originated in western China where mankind began to cultivate tea to secure a ready, reliable source. Plants of 'ancient' varieties prior to generations of natural selection or plant breeding have a genetic make up which is very diverse to enable the plant species to survive in many varied and changing conditions. For example, a plant may originate in one area but if the growing conditions change, becoming warmer or drier, the plant being unable to move locations needs to adapt or die out. Plants have a survival strategy relying on natural genetic diversity whereby new *varieties* are formed. This natural selection occurred with Camellia sinensis as there are now two main commercial varieties, the assamica variety growing in warmer lowlands and the sinensis variety growing in higher, cooler regions as previously explained.

Most people are aware that the best foods come from the best raw materials and so it is with tea that selecting the best plants is the main factor in tea flavour. Cultivating wild tea trees with a genetic diversity would produce bushes with mixed *sub-varieties* characteristics. In Japan there are still a few 'wild tree' type plantations of Camellia sinensis, without any deliberate plant breeding, being original stock native tree varieties chosen from the wild and grown together - the original Japanese tea trees came from Chinese seeds. These plantations are mixed varieties displaying bushes with different characteristics such as leaf colour, heights, yield, taste and seasonal maturity and so are difficult to farm. The method of harvest is for the farmer to regularly walk the plantation selecting and marking bushes which are ready for the picker giving some selection at the point of harvest. This tea is known as *Zairai* and is regarded by some as '*old Japan*' having a natural variable tea quality which some tea drinkers find appealing and interesting. Clearly, every zairai plantation will be different and every plucking will also be different.

Somewhere between fully cultivated plantations and wild Zairai plantations is a Chinese group of teas called *Dancong tea,* which are oolong teas from Guangdong province in southern China where a series of wild mother trees of Shuixian cultivars grew wildly all around. As these were harvested the farmers noticed certain bushes had a unique flavour so would then take cuttings from the best trees in the crop and cultivate them in single rows producing unique flavoured teas, this being plant selection and cultivation in its original form. Dancong means single stem and the leaves are now harvested from plants grown from the same mother bush so Dancong and Zairai similar, in that Zairai trees are "wild trees" all together in a plantation and spot plucked, whereas Dancong are spot selected from wild mother trees and grown separately. In the Guangdong area several different Dancong tea fragrances can be found such as almond, orchid, honey with some 'creative' names for the old trees such as Duck Shit, Old Duck, Big Dark Leaf.

Further to the above selections, the plant's natural genetics can be used to select a particular attribute that is desired. In the wild, tea grows early and late in the season, some bushes grow tall others short, and so on. If, for example, the seeds are selected only from tall plants, which are then grown and cross pollinated by sexual propagation, then tall bushes will predominate. This becomes *selective breeding* and the progeny develop into tall bushes with the small ones disappearing. Using this technique on any particular desirable trait creates a sub-variety but it takes many generations for the plant to lose the small plant genes, if at all, and the plant can revert back to a more primitive state if small plant genes lurk in the chromosomes. However, the plant will eventually 'breed out' the genes with the undesired characteristic and be unable to revert back which is why cultivated plants have a less varied genetic diversity than truly wild varieties and why some wild plants are preserved to retain genetic diversity thereby preserving the genes for possible future disease or pest resistance.

The tea plant is ever evolving with the genetic pool evolving to adapt to local conditions (terroir) so for this reason, different wild tea plantations left to sexually cross pollinate become what are known as *landraces*. They are essentially genetically similar, can interbreed easily, have become specifically adapted to local soil, climate conditions but are just a little different to each other, similar to a human 'race', and in tea these differences can usually be identified by observing the gene clusters. It is interesting to compare tea from bushes cloned by cuttings and planted in different soils and climatic region. This shows the difference that adaptation to terroir makes to the final product.

Breeding a new variety takes a long time and is expensive. Modern farming techniques use a technique called *cloning* to make a *cultivar* (**culti**vated **var**iety) which is to take many cuttings of the desirable plant which can then be be grown into new plants with the same genetic material as the mother bush. Using this technique the mother bush is exactly copied in the new generation and many copies can then be made in a reasonably quick process. For example, the *Yabukita variety* is by far the main Japanese variety and others such as Long Jing#43 used for Chinese Long Jing (Dragon Well) and Bannockburn 157 (B157), Phoobsering 312 (P312), and Ambari Vegetative 2 (AV2) which is very suitable for Darjeeling teas. Good tea is made from good quality leaves from good cultivars but even the best process cannot make poor leaves into a good tea so the choice of cultivar is crucial having the biggest effect on the finished tea.

There are hundreds of different commercial tea cultivars bred for a variety of reasons and most commercial tea is now grown by this reliable method which produces a consistent, uniform product.

So is tea growing as easy as that? – Not so! If identical cloned trees are grown in different areas they are unlikely to make the same tea as the plant becomes adapted to the area. For example, if two identical clones are taken, and one grown in a cold region and one in a hot region, the plant genetics would begin to change and the plants would become adapted to their respective environment and change the way that the genes express themselves. This is the influence of *terroir* and over time a new sub-variety could form.

The genetics of when a plant differs so much that it is a new species, landrace, variety or sub-variety is very complex but it was this very problem that exercised botanical minds for some time until it was agreed that assamica was a variety of Camellia sinensis not a different species but this was only agreed less than 200 years ago. Tea plants have great gene plasticity and change an almost infinite number of times so plant classifications are often debated as to where the line is drawn when a sub-variety becomes a new variety like the colour grey becoming a new grey or just a darker shade of the old grey.

Terroir

The story does not end with the cultivar as each cultivar has a wide flavour spectrum depending on the *terroir,* a term familiar in the wine industry, this being the set of all the environmental factors that affect a crop's characteristics or *phenotype* (traits). The plant is affected by the environment, local soil, climate, annual weather, insects and microbial flora and becomes 'adapted' for fitness to survive in a particular environment. The characteristic muscatel flavour of Darjeeling tea is attributed to a combination of the Himalayan altitude, soil conditions, direction of sun, wind and rain collectively known as the *terroir* – **the sum total of all local environmental conditions.**

G(enetics) * E(nvironment = Tea Characteristtics

Climate is critical to the development of flavour and aroma as climates that are too constant will develop less complex teas. The tea plant requires some stress to provoke defensive secondary metabolite formation, so warm days for good plant growth and cool nights to stress the plant are ideal conditions to increase the plant's internal defences and complex and unique flavours and aromas will be formed. Mountain regions display these conditions making them ideal for tea growing with some teas being grown in misty conditions where the sunlight is often reduced.

The annual weather affects final tea flavours. A study in China found extreme drought, including winter senescence, is significantly correlated with better taste and chemical concentrations but with lower tea yields compared to the monsoon harvest.

Soil is important with tea requiring acidic soil with an optimum acid soil of pH 4.5 to 5.5 which allows nutrients to be absorbed more easily. The root system of a cultivated tea bush can be about six feet deep, so soil that is loose without limestone or clay is ideal and the soil must have good drainage which is why tea gardens are often planted on hillsides. The mineral quality of the soil is also critical to the tea's metabolism, and hence the tea taste, with some oolongs being prized for their minerality taste.

Altitude plays a key role in the development of tea aromatics. High altitude puts stresses on the plant from high UV sunlit days and cold nights so develops secondary metabolites as protection leading to complex tea aromas. Growth is slow so the essential oils concentrate further. UV radiation from the sun produces UV protecting polyphenols with warm days maximising this effect, cold nights stress the plant, as does direction of slope for mists and winds, and reduced oxygen from very high altitude ,so all conditions play a role in the development of tea aromatics. Ceylon teas, for example, are divided into three main regions:-

- **Low-grown teas grown on an elevation between sea level to 600m,**
- **Mid-grown teas from 600m to 1,200m and**
- **High-grown teas grown at an elevation above 1,200m.**

The direction that the tea plantation faces will affect the final tea product. In Wuyi mountain range, with exactly the same cultivar, soils and climate, the tea may be different depending on whether it has been grown on a southern, western, eastern or northern slope. This is due to the tea bushes being shaded for most of the day or having full access to the suns rays. The wind direction in this mountainous region also has a large effect in that the tea bush may face direct winds or be in a sheltered area.

The season

The season of tea harvesting is extremely important to tea flavour so latitude is one of the factors in determining the speed of growth and the number of flushes (harvests) the tea plant will have. Close to the equator, tea can be harvested throughout the year. Sri Lanka (Ceylon) produces tea all year long with a flush about every 80 days but in Darjeeling tea can go dormant over the winter months. During this time of long, cool nights the tea becomes stressed and slowly produces defensive secondary metabolites, just the chemicals required for good flavoured tea. The first flush harvested after this dormant cycle, when the theanine and polyphenol contents are high, produces some of the best teas. A prime example of this is the range of flavours in different Darjeeling tea flushes. Spring harvested Darjeeling black tea will have a much lighter, green flavour with sweet, fruity notes sometimes described as muscatel, whereas a tea harvested later in the year will have a stronger chocolate, robust flavour.

Increased rain following the spring drought results in an increase of up to 50% in tea leaf growth and a decrease of up to 50% concentration of catechin secondary metabolites but with increased antioxidant activity. This is due to a high concentration of flavour chemicals forming in the leaf from the dormant period butwhen the rains come and the plant grows fast, they are then diluted by the rapid increase in leaf size and water content but many smaller compounds are produced with less tea taste impact. Higher sunshine during the dry season and lower sunshine hours during the monsoon season is another reason for the accumulation of particular phytochemicals in tea shoots. Tea leaves in early spring, or drought, will have more flavour than teas after the rains when growth starts as the yield of tea leaves is greater. Methylxanthines (caffeine) concentrations of tea samples harvested in north eastern India were highest during the early harvest of the dry spring season, lowest during the monsoon season, and improved with the autumn harvest. If tea is consumed for taste then spring teas before the rains are best, but if consumed for health reasons, namely antioxidant effects, then after the rains may be better – and less expensive!

For these very important reasons, Chinese teas harvested before the Qing Ming festival are highly sought after and are referred to as *Ming Qian teas*. The Qing Ming festival occurs on the first day of the fifth period of the lunar calendar, which is usually April 5th (April 4th on leap years), often referred to as

"Tomb Sweeping Day". Green teas made from leaves picked before this date are given the prestigious *pre-qingming* designation commanding a much higher price. "Grain Rain" (Gu Yu) is the sixth solar term in the 24 solar terms and the last solar term in spring starts on April 20th (Grain Rain Day) and ends on May 5th. The Grain Rain signals a rapid rise in temperature and rainfall. The tea picked on the period of Grain Rain is named *Grain Rain tea, Yu Qian, or mid-spring tea* and in some Chinese folk legends a dead man could come back to life after drinking Grain Rain tea, so worth giving it a try - if it is possible for the dead to drink *sic!* The China Tea Science Society have asked for the Grain Rain Day to be regarded as National Tea Drinking Day.

To summarise:-

> - **Pre-Qingming or Ming Qian - late March to the day of Qing Ming (April 4th or April 5th).**
>
> - **Pre-Guyu or Yu Qian - the day of Qing Ming to the day of Gu Yu around April 20th.**
>
> - **Post-Gu yu - after the rain**

In India *first flush spring Darjeeling tea* is highly sought after and commands a high price compared with the summer and autumnal flush and the same being true in Japan where the prized first flush Sencha of the season is called *shincha (new tea) or ichibancha (first tea)*. Although spring teas are highly sought after and expensive they are not exclusive to good tea as some very good summer and autumn teas testify but, all thing being equal, spring teas deliver wonderful tea. The tea flavour changes in character throughout the year becoming a 'stronger' and bolder' flavour.

Shading

An example of this occurs in production of Japanese green teas where the tea bushes are deliberately shaded which increases the level of theanine and chlorophyll. Shading produces more chlorophyll to capture the lower sunlight available, more amino acids/proteins are then formed to keep the plant biologically active and there is also a change and reduction in the type of polyphenols as the need for sunscreening is less. More amino acids also means a decrease in caffeine content as theanine and other amino acids are not converted to caffeine which uses the nitrogen from proteins. In nature, some shading may be naturally provided by surrounding mountains, or mist, but in Japan the tea grower will place a large net over the tea field to control the amount of shade on leaves.

Summarising, tea leaves grown in shade for longer periods of time will have higher levels of chlorophyll and amino acids so will be brighter green in colour. There will be less caffeine and polyphenols meaning the taste is less bitter and less astringent but with more *umami* (savoury) flavour. From the amino acids.

Tea Plantation - Image by dae jeung kim from Pixabay

CHAPTER FIVE

BIOLOGY OF TEA FLAVOURS

Tea is the combination of soluble chemicals metabolised in the leaves which contribute to tea flavour, taste, colour and mouthfeel. An understanding of plant biology is helpful to explain the reasons for these chemicals being present in tea which are all about plant survival. Tea production - from the plant, what the grower can do, through manufacture and to the infusion conditions in the cup - is about manipulating these chemicals to give an optimum tea flavour. Tea plant cultivars, agricultural practices and processing methods are employed to manipulate plant chemicals to change the balance of tea flavour and science is now helping us to understand these chemical changes to help produce the best teas. To appreciate these metabolites it is helpful to understand their role, of which the quantity, variety and potency depends on a number of factord in the plant's life.

Defence

A leaf munching insect mixes leaf chemical substrates and enzymes to produce bitter repellent chemicals other insects have sap sucking abilities where they pierce the plant stems to access the plant's nutritious sap thus avoiding the immediate bitter tasting defences. The plant then developed another line of defence by producing repellent aromatic compounds to deter such pests as the predators deliver effector molecules, specific proteins, that attenuate plant defence responses. The strategy is then for the plant to respond to insect attack by producing specific *volatile organic chemicals* (VOC), such as *aromatic terpenes*, which are released by an enzyme unlocking the odour molocule from it's benign state and releasing it into the atmosphere. The gaseous aroma released discourages the insects, such as aphids, but may also encourage another class of insects to assist the plant such as ladybirds, an aphid predator. Insect diversification created a major selective force in flowering plant evolutionary diversification, and co-existance evolved[3]. Those species that were repelled evolved ways around the plant defences, such as toleration for the bitter chemicals, requiring the plant, under evolutionary pressure to come up with other chemicals to fight the new insects. This competition gives rise to co-evolution of new species of insects and plants as defences become overcome and new ones formed. This is the insect/plant war where each use novel strategies to overcome each other's defences. The biological phenomenon of an organism producing chemicals that influence other organisms, is known as *allelopathy* and allelochemicals can be used with repellent effect on the target organisms (*negative allelopathy*) as toxins, repellants or reducing plant digestibility, or beneficial effects (*positive allelopathy*) by attracting insects for pollination or the herbivore predators to the tea plant.

Some aroma chemicals are present to attract insects as in the case of a perfumed rose attracting insects for pollination. Clearly, for a gaseous compound to be effective it must be released into the atmosphere and if this occurrs constantly the plant would need to give its limited resources to continual production of these chemicals exhausting them and also affecting natural plant growth and development. The plant has an effective way of conserving these valuable resources in the form of *glycosides* which are molecules of sugar bound to another functional non-sugar chemical groups, such as a fragrance chemical (Volatile Organic Chemical -VOC). Storing the chemical in an inactive form enables the plant to store these compounds ready for use only when necessary as the scent is locked in until required. These plant defences are called *phytoanticipins*[19] as when the plant detects a threat then enzymes (some called *glycosidases*) break down the chemical bonding between a sugar molecule and the volatile aromatic chemical and release the aroma into the atmosphere.

Catechins and terpenes may be bound up as glycosides in the cell vacuole and released from the sugar molecue when the cell breaks down and the appropriate enzymes come into contact. Chemicals which are immediately effective are called *phytoalexins*[19] and include terpenes and alkaloids such as caffeine.

This raises an interesting aspect of tea chemicals, not widely known - the flavour of tea which we find so appealing is made by the tea plant for such delightful purposes as insecticide, herbicide, fungicide, mammallian predator neurotoxins, slug repellant and sunscreen, all of which are fortunately not targetted at humans but can be useful. The chemical cocktail has evolved to be quite specific in targetting organisms an example is caffeine ingestion which can kill a dog but is harmless to a human. (This is truly – 'One man's meat is another man's poison'). This metabolite cocktail acts as both defence and plant survival and it can be argued that the tea plant is so attractive to humans that we are influenced to ensure tea plant survival by agricultural nurturing and protection. - Positive allelopathy in action!

Age

The older the tea plant the more it will have been exposed to stress and the genes responsible for a variety of defensive compounds will be activated leading to a cocktail of defensive compounds present. Ancient trees (gushu) will have a more complex flavour than young trees due to the greater variety of these chemicals produced over its lifetime. The quantity and variety of functional chemicals in tea is believed to be related to the *plant apparency hypothesis*[13], which states that a plant will invest heavily in defences when the plant is easily found, or apparent, to attacking organisms (insects, moulds, bacteria etc. both above and below the ground), so the more attack the tree has had over its lifetime the greater the defensive metabolite content of the leaves. This hypothesis is controversial but it appears that the chemical increase is qualitative

47

rather than quantitative in herbaceous plants but the reverse in woody trees, examples of which include long-living trees and shrubs such as Camellia where ancient trees over 1000 years old can be found, particularly in the Yunnan province in China.

Many explanations are given for the complex flavour of 'old tree tea (gushucha). The common explanation seems is to link the complex flavours to the depth of the roots and the effects of fertilisation from decaying leaves from the mineral rich surrounding forest trees. This is questionable as there is no evidence that the roots are significantly deeper between a 50, 100, 200 or 400 year old tree but the latter is more highly sought after (age is also a Confucian tradition). A more credible explanation, without denying the terroir effects of deep roots, is due to the fact that the tree has been around long enough to have experienced many biotic and abiotic stresses so has built up a bank of secondary chemicals and a genetic make up such that the genes are ready to express different defence chemicals and hence tea flavour. The tree will have gene architecture ready for the various attacks suffered through the plant's life and have a bank of chemicals both quantitative and qualitative.

Communication and signalling.

Plants are sessile, cannot move, and unable to avoid a predator but need to be ready for a nearby threats. Plants can signal to other parts of the same plant, such as other leaves, or neighbouring plants through the mechanism of releasing gaseous compounds into the atmosphere to alert other plants called *induced resistance*. This research is in its infancy but the premise is that the crop protects itself from threats gaining a foothold by signalling neighbouring plants to change their phenotype to be ready for this potential threat. To illustrate one plant signalling effect, bananas ripen when one banana emits ethylene, which acts as a ripening hormone, so if one ripe banana is placed amongst unripe bananas the ripening process will be accelerated in all the bananas, this also applies to tomato ripening. This leads to the tea from a bug bitten plantation being affected but not necessarily each leaf, or even each plant, will need to be attacked for the plant to express the chemical response to defend itself.

Genes

The question is why does the plant not repel all threats before they attack. Production of defensive secondary metabolites will adversly affect normal growth of the plant. Each variety of tea will have a different *genotype,* or hereditary information, but many of the potential defensive traits will not be immediately realised because of the trade off between growth and protection. If the plant put it's scarce resources into every potential threat it would not be able to grow or survive as there is a trade off between growth and protection. There are parts of the DNA code genotype that make a particular trait, be it leaf colour, shape or manufature of a particular chemical, but not all of these traits are realised all the time so plant resources can be targetted effectively by the genes responsible for a particular attribute being be turned on, or expressed, when the threat is present. Whilst the genotype may be the same for a particular cultivar, the expression of the genes will be different depending on the local threats and this expression of an observable property is called the *phenotype.* Different copies of a clone can therefore have an exact genotype – copy of full hereditary information of traits – but a different phenotype or expressions of those traits. Once a gene is 'turned on' it remains ready for some time, for example, making the leaf less edible to a herbivore even when the herbivore is no longer present, thus enabling the plant to repel a seasonal threat and be ready for the same threat in subsequent years. This is *stress imprint,* memory like properties, which are created by gene changes, making the plant ready for a repeat attack, an effect similar to mammallian antibodies. The plant does this by up or downregulating

49

gene expression so an efficient proactive defence mechanism is built up in the plant by reallocation of resources[19]. Camellia sinensis is very strongly influenced by its envirnment due to its gene architecture and this effect is called *phenotypic plasticity* meaning these gene changes occurr regularly as the plant developes survival fitness.

These phenotype changes can lead to permanent genetic changes and a landrace being created which is due to the natural changes the plant makes to adapt into its surroundings thereby increasing the plant's fitness for survival. Possible permanent genetic variation has been observed between branches of a single eucalyptus specimen where herbivory resistance was present in only one branch[12] and may be indicative of plant permanent evolutionary adaptive advantage.

The chemicals in the leaf are present through a mixture of genetics and environment so different locations produce different teas from the same clone, being the basis of *'terroir'* and *'landrace'*. The environment (terroir) in which the tea plant grows is very influential but the cultivar being the main tea taste driver and terroir a close second, the phenotype being a product of genetics (G) and environment (E) – (G*E).

The more the tea plant is **stressed** the greater the variety of defensive (tea flavour) chemicals, the greater the quantities of these chemicals and the more genetic differences present. Therefore, a very stressed plant has the potential to give a much more complex flavoured tea but perhaps having a lower yield.

Natural mutations

There are also natural, usually neutral, mutations which occur spontaneously as DNA replication errors inevitably happen during cell division. The cell division occurs in the meristem cells which are the cells at the growing tip of the bud. An accumulation of mutations throughout the life of the plant will eventually result in genetic instability or mutational meltdown, a phenomenon known as *Muller's ratchet*[10] which puts the plant at risk from a form of tree cancer. An ancient tree 200 years old will have ~10% mutant initials whereas a tree 500 years old will have ~25% mutant initials[12] so the older the tree the more mutations it is likely to have experienced. The main branch of a plant grows from the *apical* meristem (main growing tip) where the DNA copying errors can occur, but where the meristem splits to produce an axillary bud (side shoot) one mutated cell may divide and affect the apical branch (main stem), the new axial branch (side shoot) or both depending on the location of the mutated cell in the growing tip. The mutated cells divide and grow an affected branch but cannot affect those lower down the stem. Each side branch can later be subject to its own individual mutations but it does follow that the younger the branch the less the errors[10]. When the multiple mutations on a particular growing branch become too great, causing genetic instability, mutational meltdown can occur but the tree has evolved a mechanism to isolate defective or diseased tissue into a 'woody compartment' with the affected branch dying back to a healthy side branch so the rest of the tree can continue healthy growth. This mechanism, called *induced abscission*, protects the main tree enabling the very long life of trees. The tree thus has some protection against potentially destructive and accumulated mutations. This effect can be seen by gardeners when a sport occurs on a plant that may affect one branch or the whole plant. If the sport is a lethal type, but only on one branch, the branch will die back to the main stem and the rest of the plant continue healthy growth.

It also follows that different branches of the same plant may have slightly different DNA (genotype) so cloning a particular bush and then cloning the daughter bushes is like taking repeated photocopies of a photocopy of a picture where each time a copy is copied it becomes less like the original – also clones taken from an ancient mother plant may have a slightly different genotype from different mutations on different branches. Qi Dan original tea trees (see Chapter 9) were cloned to make a plantation at Bei Dou. However, the trees from which the cuttings were taken were not only originally sexually propogated, so of mixed genetics, but the cuttings taken from one particular tree may have been different to each other. When these daughter trees were further cloned they are likely to have become increasingly different to the original Qi Dan mother bushes. Bei Dou wulong tea may have no enhanced qualities than other teas in the area other than provenance. Gardeners observe these mutations on their plants and call them *sports,* examples being a white flower on an otherwise red flower plant.

Summary

Tea is a leaf that contains many soluble chemicals which are responsible for tea flavours and enjoyment. In order to defend itself against stress, both biotic (insects, mammals, fungus, moulds, bacteria, nematodes) and abiotic (UV light, cold, wind, heat, drought, excess water)a greater quantity and quality of defensive chemicals are formed which ultimately enhance the complexity of tea flavour. Genetic changes occur to a plant, temporarily, permanently or semi permanently which improve the plant's fitness for survival, or by natural sporadic mutations. If the genetics change on the growing tip, then a tree with many axillary branches on an old tree may have different genotypes on the same plant, important to consider when taking cuttings. Everything done to the leaf from cultivar selection, plucking, mechanically damaging, heating, drying affects flavour complexity due to quantity and quality of the chemical cocktail in tea. Tea flavour will be influenced by chemical defensive responses, gene expression, cell mutations and terroir threats and accumulating these changes means ancient trees make complex tasting teas - **age above beauty!**

52

CHAPTER SIX

CHEMICALS IN TEA

There are thousands of chemical compounds, which contribute to tea flavour and which can be divided into two groups to help understand their role in the plant:-

- *Primary metabolites* present in the live tea plant and necessary for growth and cell reproduction.

- *Secondary metabolites* produced from complex biochemical reactions under special circumstances for reasons such as defence, being herbivore toxic, repellant or antimicrobial, or abiotic defence such as excessive UV radiation, hot, cold, damage or drought conditions. They are not necessary for plant growth so the resource the plant gives to these chemicals detracts from normal growth which is why some are stored inactive and produced 'when necessary in response to plant attack.

Metabolites can be further divided into:-

- *Volatile organic compounds* (VOC) - contribute to tea aroma.

- *Non-volatile* compounds - these contribute to tea taste or texture.

Secondary metabolites can also be characterized as either *qualitative or quantitative.*

- Qualitative metabolites - toxins present in plants in relatively low concentrations, often less than 2% dry weight, that interfere with herbivore metabolism and are usually small, water-soluble molecules which can be rapidly synthesized, transported and stored with relatively little energy cost to the plant, examples being alkaloids such as caffeine or nicotine. Often these alkaloids can kill the predator.

- Quantitative metabolites - present in high concentration in plants ~5-40% dry weight. They are typically large molecules, so energetically expensive to produce and maintain, take longer to synthesize and transport and usually deter but do not kill the predator, examples being catechins and tannins.

There are three major sub-groups of flavour secondary metabolites:

1. Nitrogen compounds. Often alkaloids which often have pharmacological effects on humans e.g. Caffeine. Traditionally, alkaloids are defined as heterocyclic nitrogen compounds made from amino acids. Alkaloids repel and sometimes kill the predator.

2. Polyphenols (tannins. catechins or complex flavenoids) are the most common and widespread group of defensive compounds of which some have antiseptic, sunscreening or antioxidant properties.

3. Terpenes which contain volatile essential oils e.g. Citronella, limonene, jasmone (all present in tea) and also camphor and menthol. Some terpenes have an odour which can be used to repel predators such as sucking insects and encourage others to aid pollination.

These chemicals give tea its characteristic flavour often with pharmacological properties. Some are safely stored in the plant vacuole and only become active when the plant is under threat, for example when the cell membrane is punctured and they can come into contact with the enzymes in the cell cytoplasm. This is like those light sticks that only glow when the glass tube inside the plastic tube is broken and the enzyme mixes with the substrate to cause fluorescence. We now explore what these chemicals are and why the tea plant expends so much resource making them.

Organoleptic Tea Chemicals

The major chemicals in tea with a large influence on the flavour[9,10,11] :- of tea are:-

- **Caffeine - A bitter alkaloid**

- **Catechins/tannins - Bitter, astringent**

- **Polyphenols/Terpenes - Flowery, fruity**

- **Theanine – Savoury/Umami/Umami**

The major primary chemicals in tea with a large influence on the colour of tea are:-

- **Theaflavins – Yellow/brown**

- **Thearugbigins – Red/brown**

- **Flavonol – Pale yellow**

- **Chlorophylls – Green**

Alkaloids

Xanthine: $R_1 = R_2 = R_3 = H$

Caffeine: $R_1 = R_2 = R_3 = CH_3$

Theobromine: $R_1 = H$, $R_2 = R_3 = CH_3$

Theophylline: $R_1 = R_2 = CH_3$, $R_3 = H$

Wikipedia – Caffeine (1,3,7-trimethixanthine) Methylxanthines

Caffeine is a white crystalline methylxanthine alkaloid present in tea at 2-4% responsible for the bitter taste in tea. Methylxanthines also include theophylline and theobromine which are molecules rich in nitrogen, an element that may be scarce in the rain drenched mountainous terrain where tea grows. Global consumption of caffeine has been estimated at 120,000 tonnes per year, making it the world's most popular psychoactive substance. The caffeine content in a cup of tea ranges between 20-70mg per 170ml cup from around 2.5g of tea leaves, but depends on infusion time and the type of tea. A cup of coffee, in comparison, has 40–155mg of caffeine per 170ml or roughly twice that of tea.

Caffeine is the major purine alkaloid in tea and is stored in the cell vacuole where it is complexed with polyphenols acting as a feeding deterrent to insects and mammals partly due to its bitterness but mainly its neurotoxic properties. To protect the plant it is a natural, effective pesticide neurotoxin for insects, slugs and snails, some other invertebrates and spiders - causing spiders to lose the ability to spin a proper web – and is also toxic for fungi. This latter property is particularly important in Ceylon where the shot-hole borer beetle is a tea pest which symbiotically depends on a wood-rotting fungus to provide the ambrosia it needs to survive. The caffeine in the tea plant provides an efective means to control this pest by controlling the fungus on which it feeds. Additionally, caffeine also includes autotoxic properties which means it inhibits the growth of seedlings in the soil, including those of the mother plant, as the decaying leaf litter releases caffeine which protects the plants nutrient base from competition. It is so effective at this that Camellia sinensis has become an invasive pest species in a nature reserve in Tanzania.

Caffeine has both a negative and positive allelopathy properties depending on the dose. Recently, in 2015, theanine, the amino acid marker for Camellia sinensis, was found in honey meaning it originated from the nectar of Camellia sinensis which also contains small doses of caffeine[5]. It is thought that caffeine activates the brains of honey bees enhancing their long term memory[14] so the bees become more likely to remember the scent of the flower and preferentially seek the nectar of those flowers that possess caffeine revisiting the flowers to spread its pollen further[7]. Insects feeding on nectar containing caffeine get a beneficial buzz! - so caffeine has a secondary advantage of positve allelopathy by attracting honeybees[6]. For humans caffeine is a bitter tasting chemical which is toxic at high doses but beneficially affects our brains at low doses as it readily crosses the blood-brain barrier causing a pleasant stimulating effect on the central nervous system and aiding wakefulness.

Caffeine levels decrease with the maturity of the leaves but increase when the cell amino acids break down providing the nitrogen to make caffeine. This appears logical as the dying cell no longer needs the amino acids to build proteins but by utilising the nitrogen within the amino acids to make caffeine the mother plant is being protected.

Polyphenols

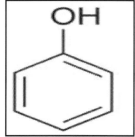

Polyphenols are some of the major sources of flavour compounds in tea. On the left is phenol, the building block of polyphenols (many phenols). This phenol structure is widely found in metabolic chemicals as each phenol molecule can have a different molecule attached to each of the six corners and these phenol structures can further be assembled together like jigsaw pieces to form larger complex molecules each having different proprties, such as tea taste as seen in the chemicals catechin and gallocatechin gallate below where another polyphenol structure has been added to the catechin molecule to form epigallocatechin gallate, teas best antioxidant.

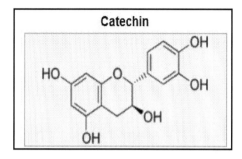

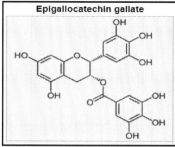

Wikipedia

The main flavour water soluble constituents of tea leaves belong to the polyphenol group [18] accounting for a massive 25-35% on a dry weight basis, a tea drinker typically consuming ~180-240 mg of polyphenols from a strong cup of tea. Polyphenols, mainly catechins imn tea, contribute to the bitterness, astringency and sweet aftertaste of tea. Their properties in the plant deters insect munching, by their repellent bitterness, and some act as a sunscreen to filter out potentially damaging UVB light. Many polyphenols are present in the leaf and others are created when enzymes comes into contact with the polyphenols compounds. Some are synthesised from amino acids via sunlight meaning shaded tea bushes, either artificially screened or naturally from mist or plantation direction, have a smaller concentration of polyphenols present in the leaf and a higher concentration of amino acids.

Polyphenols are a wide chemical grouping and within this group is a class of compounds called flavonoids which number ~4000. Within this flavonoid group are the flavanols and within flavanols are groups of flavonols and catechins. (Note the confusing spelling *flavanol* and *flavonol*). These groupings represent metabolic pathways with the groups below become smaller from left to right as the molecules get larger.

Polyphenols - Flavonoids - Flavanols - Flavonols - Catechins[a] - Tannins

Tea is particularly rich in three flavonoid classes: flavan-3-ols (catechins), oligimeric flavonoids[b] (including thearubigins and theaflavins generated during fermentation), and flavonols (eg,quercetin)

(a) Catechins (flavan-3-ols)

Catechin, epicatechin, epicatechin gallate, epigallocatechin, gallocatechin, epigallocatechin gallate (EGCG).

These are catechins of great importance in tea being powerful antioxidants and the source of the many health claims surrounding tea, but EGCG is the largest, most powerful antioxidant and most researched of them all in green tea. Flavan-3-ols are insect feeding deterrents contributing to the bitterness, astringency and sweet aftertaste of tea.

In humans, salivary proline-rich proteins are secreted in the oral cavity which precipitate (come out of solution) when they bind with tannins which are massive polyphenol complex chemicals in tea,. Tannins causes astringency which is a physical drying or puckering of the mouth, for example, tasting red wine or stewed tea causes thickening of saliva and mouth drying wich is the proline/tannin complex . Tannins are found in a variety of foods such as coffee, beer, strawberries, bananas and raspberries.

The action of chewing, or macerating a tea leaf during tea manufacture, breaks the cell walls and allows contact between the catechins in the vacuole and an enzyme called *polyphenol oxidase* in the cell cytoplasm which causes enzymatic oxidation of catechins to *theaflavins* (orange brown) *and thearubigins* (reddish brown). Thearubigins are condensation products of oxidised catechins with theaflavins. These compounds are deliberately created in black tea manufacture being responsible for the colour and heavy robust flavours sometimes described as chocolate or malt compared to the light fragrances of the unoxidised chemicals. This oxidation effect that can be witnessed when an apple or banana is cut and the surface exposed to oxygen in the air turns the fruit brown. The yellow colour in green tea infusion is mainly determined by the water soluble flavonols (flavus -Latin for yellow). This oxidation is the main reaon why green tea has ~30% catechins and black oxidised tea has only ~4%.

The bud and first leaf have the highest concentration of polyphenols which decrease in each leaf moving down the plant as the plant is protecting the new, delicate and developing growth. An important function of polyphenols is screening against UVB light as they are powerful UVB filters as sunlight which is necessary to sustain life is be very damaging to cells, however, strangely polyphenols would be expected to occur predominantly in the epidermal (skin) cells but oddly they are concentrated in the vacuoles of mesophyll cells with little or none in the epidermis. Based on documented beneficial effects of green tea on mouse skin models many pharmaceutical and cosmetic companies are supplementing their skin care products with green tea extracts very much for this UVB screening property.

(b) Thearubigins and Theaflavins

Black tea colour and flavour is formed during the enzymatic oxidation and condensation (joining) of epigallocatechin and epigallocatechin gallate by polyphenol oxidase enzymes and in the process two major groups of pigments, *theaflavins* (yellow) and *thearubigins* (reddish brown) are formed both being powerful antioxidants and also responsible for the staining effect of tea. Dry black tea contains 99 times more theaflavins and 45 times more thearubigins than green tea[20]. Theaflavins (yellow orange) give astringency, briskness, brightness and colour of the tea beverage comprising a number of fractions of theaflavin monogallate and digallate, epitheaflavic acid and iso-theaflanin. The chemical structure is massive as polyphenols join together to form very complex compounds.

![Chemical structures of (--)-Theaflavin and Theaflavin 3'-gallate]

(--)-Theaflavin   Theaflavin 3'-gallate

Kunisuke Izawa, Motonaka Kuroda, - Comprehensive Natural Products II

Terpenes/Terpenoid compounds

Terpenes are a large and diverse class of organic compounds produced by a variety of plants for allelopathy reasons. The basic structure is built up from isoprene building blocks "head to tail" forming chains or rings leading to complex organic chemicals such as aroma chemicals, steroids and carotenes. This is again nature taking a simple chemical and using this like a jigsaw to make more complex chemicals.

Isoprene   Nerolidol (ginger, jasmine, lavender, lemon grass)

The main difference between terpenes and terpenoids is that terpenes are hydrocarbons (C-H) whereas terpenoids have been oxidised (C-H-O) which occurs in black teas. These compounds are responsible for aroma chemicals which are commercially useful for their aromatic, perfume and taste qualities

61

playing a role in many traditional herbal remedies and are often called *essential oils*. A few significant examples of aromatic terpenes in tea are citronellal, citronellol, geraniol, linaool and linalool oxides, and these compounds are also found in rose oil. There are thousands of terpenoids, many with significant aromatic, fruity, flowery properties contributing to tea flavour and these chemicals are important to the tea plant as an insect repellant or attractant - geraniol, for example, is known to be an effective mosquito repellant and has been considered an insect repellent ingredient since ~1999 but also produces a sweet smell similar to roses and is a popular choice for many bath and body products. Many of these compounds possess alleged health benefits to humans with many herbal infusions relying on this class of compounds an exapmple being citronella oil which is used extensively in perfumery.

Linalool, responsible for sweetness, has been shown to be an effective insecticide against fruit flies, fleas and cockroaches and the Environmental Protection Agency has approved linalool as a pesticide, flavour agent and scent and use in a wide variety of bath and body products. It is interesting to note that our lovely smelling bath oils may actually be insecticides!

Not all terpenes are floral or fragrant. Quercetin, abundant in nature is bitter and the most prominent flavonol in tea[20] so tea contains caffeine, catechins and quercetin as bitter compounds. Unlike the other two quercetin is not water soluble so does not significantly contribute to tea flavour, however, matcha tea which is consumed whole as a powdered leaf with the drink can taste very bitter partly because of quercetin which is reputed to be a powerful chemical beneficial to health.

Amino acids (proteins)

Amino acids, like the complex compounds above are the building blocks of proteins where a simple structure links in chains to form a long protein molecule. Tea contains many amino acids and a significant amount of protein which makes up 6% of the extract solids in steeped tea and gives tea its brothiness. Amino acids contribute to tea flavours both individually and also react with carbohydrates in the tea manufacturing process to provide other flavours. Proteins can form a complex with polyphenols to create astringency which is described as mouthfeel or drying of the saliva.

Many amino acids on their own contribute to flavour but their role is not fully understood so much research is being undertaken on the interaction between amino acids and human taste receptors. Some, such as arginine and alanine, contribute to a sweet taste, others are bitter tasting, whilst glutamates have no flavour of their own but have taste enhancing properties. These cause other flavours to exceed the taste properties of the compounds on their own, monosodium glutamate (msg) being a familiar food additive example making meaty flavours more meaty.

Theanine, more specifically L-Theanine (γ-glutamylethylamide), is the most abundant amino acid in tea accounting for 50% of the total amino acids (3%). It is a non-protein amino

acid unique to the tea plant meaning that it only exists in the free form. The umami (savoury) taste of green tea infusion has been shown to be due to some amino acids, in particular theanine, which is a relatively uncommon amino acid being found in very few plants such as Camellia sinensis, shitake mushrooms, a mushroom called Boletus badius and a plant called guayusa. The function in the plant of this amino acid in tea is not fully understood but is unique to the Theaceae family groupof plants. Theanine is found in all parts of the tea plant being synthesised in the root and accumulating in young and active tissues and also younger plants emphasising its metabolic role in the tea plant. The distribution of theanine in the shoots indicated that the first leaf is the principal site for the synthesis of polyphenolic compounds from theanine showing the benefit of the 'bud and two leaves' principle for tea plucking to obtain maximum tea flavours.

Theanine imparts a characteristic *umami* flavour in tea which is one of the five basic tastes detected by the tongue, the others being sweetness, saltiness, sourness, bitterness. It has been described as savoury and is characteristic of broths and cooked meats. People taste umami through taste receptors that typically respond to glutamates widely present in meat broths and fermented products and are commonly added to some foods in the form of monosodium glutamate (MSG). Since umami has its own receptors, rather than arising out of a combination of the traditionally recognized taste receptors, scientists now consider umami to be a distinct taste and since 1985 the term umami was recognized as the scientific term to describe the taste of glutamates. There is also another property of theanine, descovered quite recently called *kokumi*[7]. Kokumi substances increase the intensity of the taste signals on the tongue such that sugar solutions taste sweeter and salt solutions taste saltier.

Theanine, very significantly, has a mitigating effect on caffeine stimulation as it also able to cross the blood–brain barrier where it has a calming effect. Caffeine stimulates to the point where caffeine drinks, such as coffee, lead to caffeine highs and twitchiness, whereas with theaninecalming the mind, the tea drinker is lifted by caffeine and calmed by theanine at the same time setting in a state of relaxed alertness. L-theanine significantly increases activity in the alpha frequency band[22] which indicates that it relaxes the mind without inducing drowsiness. However, this effect has only been established at higher doses than that typically found in a cup of black tea (approximately 20mg). Alpha activity is known to play an important role in critical aspects of attention with theanine being most effective in individuals who generally have high levels of anxiety but the effect applies to everyone.

The effects of caffeine ant L-theanine in tea impart the property of creating a **'relaxed alertness'**.

Carbohydrates (Saccharides)

Carbohydrates are formed during photosynthesis being simple sugars, or chains of sugars as building blocks, making starch, cellulose and fibre both soluble and insoluble. Sugar molecules taste sweet, contributing approximately 11% to extract solids. As starches and sugars they are used in primary metabolism and, amongst other chemicals, for the creation of polyphenols in young tea leaves. They are also a component in glycosides which keep a functional metabolite inactive until required and are explained above in the terpene section. Glucosides are glycosides where the sugar molecule is glucose.

Organic Acids

Organic acids play an essential role in aroma formation in tea. Tea is a significant source of citric, tartaric, malic, oxalic, fumaric and succinic acids detected in Assam leaf. These acids have their own tate but acids and alcohols combine together to create esters and these have aroma properties contributing to tea flavour.

Minerals

Minerals constitute about 4-9% of the inorganic matter of tea with significant amounts of fluorine, potassium, magnesium, and calcium. The unusually high amount of fluorine due, in part, to the uptake of aluminum fluoride is found in greater amounts in older tea leaves and helps to prevent tooth decay but minerals do not impact significantly on flavour.

Pigments

Chlorophyll is the green colour in the infused leaf and the infusion colour of green tea is mainly determined by the chlorophyll content and the ratio of *chlorophyll A* which is dark green, to *chlorophyll B* which is yellowish-green. During oxidation chlorophylls degrade to olive grey pheophytins so the green colouration is lost in oxidised teas. Tea grown in the shade has been found to have increased levels of chlorophyll, as the plant is trying to capture as much sunlight as possible to power its metabolism, and carotenoids which later assist in aroma production and, with the lower quantity of catechins, results in a less astringent beverage.

Carotenoids are bright yellow/orange compounds responsible for the colour of carrots and rustic leaf shades, the four major carotenoids being ß-carotene, lutein, violaxanthine and neoxanthine [11]. They are present in the leaf but their presence is overpowered by chlorophyll until it breaks down and they become noticeable as happens in the autumn. Some sweet floral smells in black tea and many fruits are due to the aromatic compounds resulting from carotenoid biochemistry and these are the terpenes described previously. These pigment chemicals in tea are present in small quantities and degrade by enzymatic and non-enzymatic oxidation to produce powerful aroma compounds and it is the abundance of double bonds in the chemical structure that absorb the UV light, and consequently affect the flavour of the finished tea particularly if solar withering is used. Carotenoid derivatives such as linalool, a typical flavour chemical in tea with lavender or citrus notes, β-damascenone with a fruity/apple flavour and β-ionone with sweet violet aroma are aroma compounds derived from carotenoid degradation[11] and are also key odour-contributing compounds in flowers so can not only be used extensively in the perfumes and fragrance industry but also an insecicide for fleas and fruit flies.

UV light in solar withering produces non-enzymatic photo-oxidation aroma compounds by degrading β-carotene, to β-ionone, and degrading phytofluene to nerolidol, having a flowry aroma, and geranylacetone also with a flowry aroma. Carotenoid derivatives are formed by oxidation so are much more abundant in black teas.

Lipids

Lipids include fatty acids and are present in tea but do not significantly contribute to flavour as primary chemicals in themselves but act as precursers for aromatic compounds such as linolenic, linoleic, oleic and palmitic acids acid producing hexanals and hexonols which are contributers to leafy, grassy aromas [11]. Hexanal and geranial, are greatly reduced in *aged* green tea as catechins react with hexanal reducing its effect, showing that poor storage of green tea has a great effect on tea taste.

Lipid degeneration of α-linolenic acid also produces fragrant volatiles, such as jasmine derivatives which are in high concentrations but have a low threshold for taste which is why jasmine pairs well with tea.

Some readers may not associate tea with fat and to explain, the fat part of the leaf keeps water outside the leaf cells and water inside the cell and it is the waxy coat that makes water droplets form on the surface of a leaf. The flavours created are from fatty acids which are nipped off the fat molecule by enzymes called lipoxygenase which are stored in the part of the cell that contains the chlorophyll called a chloroplast or from glycolipids where the sugar is nipped off the fatty acid. The more chloroplasts present the more enzyme present so early season spring tea, with a pale delicate green, contains less chloroplasts and so less lipoxygenase leading to less hexanols and a less grassy taste.

Maillard Reaction Chemicals

Secondary chemicals are compounds found in processed tea leaves are formed from compounds in the tea during the manufacturing processes. Many of these chemicals are produced during the manufacturing process rather than naturally occurring biochemical reactions. This is the area that a skilled tea maker will be manipulating to make the desired tea flavour. Some flavours come from the *Maillard reaction,* a caramelisation chemical reaction between amino acids and reducing sugars that proceeds rapidly at high temperatures from around 140-165°C and is responsible for a range of aromas and flavours in all kinds of baked and roasted foods including tea. This 'caramelisation' reaction produces brown pigments with roasted, caramel, toasty, biscuit type flavours so heat treated pan-fired green teas will contain higher levels of Maillard reaction products than steamed treated teas. Compounds are created by this reaction and these in turn, break down to form yet more flavour compounds, and so on until many different chemicals and flavours, are created. Each type of food has a very distinctive set of flavour compounds formed by the amino acids and sugars available during the Maillard reaction and it is the combination of these compounds that make the characteristic taste and colour differences between foods such as roast chicken, beef and pork. Food technologists can use this reaction, combining a recipe of different amino acids and different sugars to make artificial food flavours with high temperature being essential for this reaction to take place.

The following chemicals and flavours are produced by the Maillard reaction in tea[11] :-

- **Furan - spicy, smoky, cinnammon-like**
- **Pyrrole - sweet, slightly smoky, nutty**
- **Oxazole - sweet**
- **Thiazole - slightly smoky, coffee-like**

The point here is not merely to give examples of unfamiliar chemical names but to show that these compounds produce different flavours when tea is heat treated in the fixing and drying stages leading to a complexity of tea flavours putting emphasis on the skill of a good tea maker to achieve a consistent, balanced flavoured tea. Other flavour compounds from this reaction have been described as popcorn-like, honey-like nutty and meaty.

In order to illustrate the complexity of tea flavours, linalool comes in two chemical forms which both have the same chemical formula but the structures are mirror images of each other like a right and left hand being the same but mirror images of each other. There is R-Linalool, or licareol, which smells like lavender, and S-linalool, or coriandrol, which is sweeter and citrousy, coriander. Also, β-ionone smells of violets but the ability to smell this chemical is genetically determined so some people smell nothing at all and that includes 42% of Europeans [8].

There is also a genetic aspect involved in perceiving tea flavours as illustrated by bitter tasting. In 1931, a chemist named Arthur Fox was pouring powdered Phenylthiocarbamide (PTC) into a bottle when some of it accidentally blew into the air. A colleague nearby complained that the dust tasted bitter but Fox tasted nothing at all. Fox had his friends and family try the chemical then describe how it tasted. Some people tasted nothing and some found it intensely bitter and others thought it tasted only slightly bitter. Soon after this discovery, geneticists determined that there is an inherited component that influences how we taste PTC. Today we know that the ability to taste PTC is conveyed by a single gene that codes for a taste receptor on the tongue.

Although PTC is not found in nature, the ability to taste it correlates strongly with the ability to taste other bitter substances that do occur naturally, many of which are toxins. We already know that plants produce a variety of toxic compounds in order to protect themselves from being eaten. Our ability to discern bitter tastes evolved as a mechanism to prevent early humans from eating poisonous plants. Humans have about 30 genes that code for bitter taste receptors. Each receptor can interact with several compounds, allowing people to taste a wide variety of bitter substances. If the ability to taste bitter compounds conveys a selective advantage then non-tasters are vulnerable to poisonous plants so why do so many people still carry the non-tasting PTC variant? Some scientists believe that non-tasters of PTC can taste other bitter compounds. This scenario would give the greatest selective advantage to *heterozygotes*, or people who carry one tasting allele and one non-tasting allele.

Strict herbivores avoiding bitter plants would have severely limitted food sources so have fewer bitter taste genes than omnivores or carnivores. This would make them vulnerable to toxic plants so instead, animals that graze on plants have a high tolerance to toxins by having large livers that are able to break down toxic compounds.

Following is a useful table of tea flavour chemicals and note the precursers, for example, the precurser of nerolidaol are carotenoids so the more carotenoids present in the leaf the more nerolidaol can be formed. In reality, the biochemical pathways are very complex as some compounds are formed from one or more precursers.but does not take into account the human experience of multiple flavours. For example, if taste was a colour there may be a red flavour and a yellow flavour but together it may not be possible to distinguish individual flavours but there may be a strange orange flavour. Additionally, some bitter and astringent flavours block delicate fragrances both by overpowering the delicate floral flavour or by nerve pathway blocking.

Compounds	Precursors	Type of tea identified	Aroma quality
β-Ionone	Carotenoids	Green, Oolong, Black tea	Woody, violet
Nerolidiol	Carotenoids	Green, Oolong, Black tea	Flowery
Theaspirone	Carotenoids	Black tea	Flowery
α-Ionone	Carotenoids	Black tea	Woody, hay-like
β-Damascone	Carotenoids	Green tea	Sweet Hay-like
Sarfranal	Carotenoids	Green, Oolong, Black tea	Herbal
Geranylacetone	Carotenoids	Green, Oolong, Black tea	Floral, hay-like
β-Damascenone	Carotenoids, Glycosides	Green, Black tea	Fruity, apple-like
(Z)-3-hexenol	Lipids, Glycosides	Green, Oolong, Black tea	Green
Hexanal	Lipids	Green tea, Oolong tea, Black tea	Grassy, green
Pentanal	Lipids	Green tea	Pungent, malt, almond
(Z)-1,5-octadien-3-one	Lipids	Green tea	Geranium-like
Jasmine	Lipids	Green tea	Jasmine-like
(E,Z)-2,6-nonadienal	Lipids	Green tea	Cucumber-like
1-Octen-3-one	Lipids	Green tea	Mushroom-like
cis-Jasmone	Lipids	Green, Oolong, Black tea	Floral, jasmine-like
(Z)-4-heptanal	Lipids	Green, Oolong, Black tea	Hay-like
1-Penten-3-ol	Lipids	Oolong tea	Butter, green
(E)-2-hexenal	Lipids	Green tea, Black tea	Green
(E,E)-2,4-hexadienal	Lipids	Black tea	Fatty
(E,E)-2,4-decadienal	Lipids	Green tea, Black tea	Fatty, fried
(Z)-3-hexenal	Lipids	Green tea, Black tea	Green
Methyl jasmonate	Lipids	Green, Oolong, Black tea	Floral
Hexanoic acid	Lipids	Black tea	Sweaty, green

Compounds	Precursors	Type of tea identified	Aroma quality
2,3-Butanedione	Lipids	Green tea	Butter
(E)-geraniol	Glycosides	Green, Oolong, Black tea	Rose-like
Linalool	Carotenoids Glycosides	Green, Oolong, Black tea	Floral
Linalool Oxide I II III IV	Glycosides	Green, Oolong, Black tea	Earthy, floral, creamy
Hotrienol	Glycosides	Oolong tea	Flowery
Methyl salicylate	Glycosides	Green, Oolong, Black tea	Minty
Benzyl alcohol	Glycosides	Green, Oolong, Black tea	Burning taste, faint aromatic
2-Phenyl ethanol	Glycosides	Oolong tea, Black tea	Honey-like
4-Hydroxy-2,5-dimethyl-3(2H)-furanone	Glycosides	Black tea	Caramel-like
Dimethyl disulfide	Maillard reaction	Green tea, Oolong tea	Garlic-like
Trimethylsulfide	Maillard reaction	Black tea	Putrid
2-Acetyl-3-methylpyrazine	Maillard reaction	Black tea	Roasty
2-Ethyl-3,5-dimethylpyrazine	Maillard reaction	Black tea	Nutty
5-Ethyl-2,3-dimethylpyrazine	Maillard reaction	Black tea	Nutty
Indole	Maillard reaction	Green tea, Oolong tea	Animal-like
2-Acetyl-2-thiazoline	Maillard reaction	Black tea	Popcorn-like
2-Acetyl-1-pyrroline	Maillard reaction	Black tea	Popcorn-like
Phenyl-acetaldehyde	Maillard reaction	Oolong tea, Black tea	Honey-like
4-Methyl-2-methyl-2-butanethiol	Maillard reaction	Green tea	Meaty
4-Mercapto-4-methyl-2-pentanone	Maillard reaction	Green tea	Meaty
Methional	Maillard reaction	Green, Black tea	Potato-like

C.-T. Ho et al. / Food Science and Human Wellness 4 (2015) 9–27

Manipulating the Chemistry

Tea evolved by teamakers manipulating the leaves originally by accident and later by design. Every stage of tea produces a different chemical cocktail - the tea cultivar (genetics), the terroir (environment), the processing/manufacture and the cup preparation. The moment the leaf is plucked senescence starts and the leaf biochmistry begins to change. Starting with green tea, the leaves in harvesting and drying experience leaf edge damage noticable by edge browning caused by partial enzymatic oxidation and new fragrant oolongs are born and leaf damage part of the tea making process. Of course the amount of damage and withering conditions of humidity, temperature, wind, solar or indoor for the oxidation to take place becomes a teamakers skill in making the range of oolongs we now have. Taking damage a step further, if the whole leaf was bruised a more complete oxidation takes place and a darker tea is made which not only has a distinct flavour but stores and travels well as there is little further oxidation to take place, and the distances tea was traded by the chinese made fully oxidised black (red) teas popular outside China.

Every gardener and chef is aware that the tender shoots of a plant have the most flavour so picking just the tender white, furry buds at dawn, before the sun has raised the chlorophyll level, gives a very fragrant, delicate tasting white tea but of limited yield. If the plucking standard includes a leaf with the bud the yield is much greater but the tea still fragrant with a more intense impact so white tea can be bud only, or bud and one leaf, but is always early plucked.

Controlled ageing of tea leads to complex flavours. Hermetically sealed containers are a relatively modern invention so tea was stored in damp conditions for long periods and the people in south West China sometimes buried their tea for storage. Tea was compressed into cakes for long distance transport thereby trapping some moisture in the block. The flavour produced

73

over time by the bacteria and moulds in these cakes became something to be desired so became a deliberate process step for puerh tea by steaming the tea to add moisture prior to compression. Modern manufacture uses wet piling, putting mats over a heap of leaves, to make this process quicker and following this is storage or 'dry storage'. Liu Bao, a sister tea in this category, has damp leaves packed into sacks or baskets which naturally ferments with age. Both teas came about by accident rather than design but with the scientific knowledge now being applied to tea manufacture these teas are made by design - and these teas store well and have unique sort after flavours!

Insect damage for most crops is bad for yield and quality however,with tea, attack by insects can actually improve the quality of the cup by inducing chemical changes which improve the flavour of tea. A famous example of this is a tea called *Oriental Beauty (Dong Fan Mei Ren)* originally named *Pengfeng tea* (Bragger's Tea) where the pest leaf hopper insect's damage leads to the tea leaves producing high amounts of aromatic terpenes as a plant defence response mechanism to deter these predators. In particular monoterpene diol, hotrienol, linalool and geraniol terpenes are produced which contribute to the muscatel aroma of both oriental beauty and some top end Darjeelings, thus giving the tea its unique flavour. Discovered by accident this tea is now deliberately produced pesticide free as insects are needed to produce the flavour. The damage also causes oxidation to take place on the growing leaves turning them into an oolong type tea giving its unique fragrant flavour. Only the damaged leaves can be selected to make premium tea making this tea incredibly labour intensive from start to finish, so do try a genuine Oriental Beauty tea but beware, there are many fakes.

Another particular processed tea is called *Gaba or Gabalong (Gaba oolong)* which is an oolong tea specially processed to have high levels of the amino acid gamma amino butyric acid which imparts a distinct aroma and flavour profile.

Common descriptors include woody, pleasant fruity, sour notes, and lasting cinnamon notes. It is a relatively new type of tea, first produced in 1987 in Japan, in which almost all the glutamic acid is converted to gamma amino butyric acid without changing the content of catechin or caffeine. GABA tea is created by using freshly picked tea leaves placed in stainless steel vacuum drums which are exposed to anaerobic conditions by replacing the oxygen with nitrogen for eight to ten hours. Then oxygen is introduced and the container is shaken continuously for about three hours. These steps can be repeated several times prior to steaming causing the glutamic acid in the leaves to be converted into GABA. Further study revealed increased levels of glutamic acid in tea leaves shaded for ten to fifteen days before picking raising concentrations of GABA. GABA tea is produced according to standards set by the Japanese government, and must contain the minimum Japanese standard of 150 mg of gamma amino butyric acid per 100 grams of tea.

GABA has alleged health benefits being formed naturally in the brain where its function is to decrease neuron activity thereby preventing anxiety and stress related messages reaching the motor centres of the brain and instilling calm. However, it is disputed whether this chemical in tea passes the blood-brain barrier to have any effect, so GABA tea is a novel tea with a particular flavour profile but it is better to disregard the disputed therapeutic effects. One confirmed effect is that gamma amino butyric acid is a *bitter taste antagonist* which means that bitterness in any food is reduced by the presence of gamma amino butyric acid. There is a patent for use of GABA '*to mask or reduce the unpleasant taste impression of an unpleasantly tasting substance such as caffeine*[15]. GABA acid acts by binding the taste receptor on the tongue for bitter taste hence reducing the effective taste of bitter components such as quinine, caffeine and niringin in citrous fruits, such that it may be possible to reduce the sugar content of a food or drink by the addition of GABA.

CHAPTER SEVEN

TEA MANUFACTURE

The days of Shen Nong are well past and more is required than popping a tea bag into hot water being all that is necessary to make tea. Several thousands of years of plant development and manufacturing refinement has been applied to make tea what it is today with hundreds of different teas available in the market, but for all the thousands of years man has been making tea it is only in the last hundred years or so that the scientific community has turned its attention to understanding this process to make tea where taste prevails.

The basic full flow process of tea is:-

- **Harvesting (Plucking)**
- **Withering**
- **Bruising (Disruption)**
- **Oxidising**
- **Fixing (Heat treatment)**
- **Shaping**
- **Drying**
- **Special Further Processing**

Leaf Harvesting

Tea production starts with harvesting the leaves either by hand plucking or machine. The decision of hand plucking or machine harvesting depends on cost and availability of labour, the terrain, size of plantation and the type of tea being made. If the leaves are harvested for a high-end tea, it is usually manual giving the greatest care to the leaf as machine harvesting is non-selective and damages the leaf leading to uncontrolled oxidation This is not too much of a problem for oxidised teas but harms the delicate balance of fragrances in unoxidised white and green teas.

Image by Quang Nguyen vinh from Pixabay

Picking the bud is important to tea plant health and yield of the tea bush. Whilst the bud at the tip of a branch, called the apical bud, is still intact it prevents side buds (axillary buds) growing by producing hormones known as auxins. This effect is known as *apical dominance* and the effect lasts until the apical bud is either removed or the distance from the apical bud to the axillary bud is too great for the auxin to be effective. When the apical bud is removed by plucking, the dormant axillary bud below, or sometimes two or three buds, are then able to grow and the plant will bush out creating many more branches each with an apical bud. A group of shoots of the same maturity on the plant is called a *generation* and when these are plucked it is called a *flush*. After a plucking session the new shoots are allowed to grow and then harvested in the next or second, flush. In Darjeeling, India, there are three distinct flushes, spring, summer and autumn, giving teas of very different characteristics. Correct plucking takes the tasty tips of the plant and also encourages side shoots to develop thereby increasing the yield of the plant

Plucking is the first step in making a quality tea and requires a defined bud/leaf configuration called a *plucking standard*. The plucking standard that most people are familiar with is 'two leaves and a bud', this being the original plucking standard for quality green tea going back to at least the Tang dynasty (618-907AD). Sometimes the bud and one leaf is plucked for Huangshan Mao Feng, sometimes three leaves and the tip, no bud, is harvested for Tie Guan Yin and sometimes a fourth leaf is plucked for souchong teas. Regular picking is necessary to generate fresh growth and avoid the volatile flavour compounds imparting excessive grassy, green flavour to tea which can increase with long plucking intervals. Additionally, an even pluck and careful handling of the leaves by the pickers is required so that the leaf generation is as close as possible to ensure an even batch of tea for processing. The bud is the part of the plant which is growing and will contain the highest concentration of flavour compounds so, for this reason, it is very important in tea plucking.

White tea sometimes requires only buds to make this delicately fragrant tea so requires special hand plucking to minimise any damage and uncontrolled oxidation. One Chinese emperor of an ancient dynasty, was given this as tribute tea that was untouched by human hands and plucked by virgins with golden scissors into a golden bowl but, for some strange reason, this plucking standard is seldom used! Whlist not being sure of the status of the 'lady pickers', this tea picked using white gloves and golden scissors can be obtained from a French Tea Company, Mariage Freres, but it is from a Ceylon plantation and cost £25 per cup in 2010!

In Henan province, Gushi county West Jiuhua Shan scenic area, a specialized collection tool called a"tea willow basket" is sometimes used by pickers when picking leaves with their mouths to make Kou Chun Cha ("Mouth Lip Tea"). This tool is made from Xinyang's famous weaved willow wood and is placed between the breasts during use to receive the tender tea leaves that the female tea-leaf picker plucks with her mouth. New pickers were recently being sought with adverts specifying that 'applicants must be virgins' and offering payment of £50 a day. They must also have at least a C-cup bra size – virginity and curviness, believed to promote well-being and purity. How about that for political correctness! Regrettably, I have not been able to source this tea myself but it is reported that tourism in this region has increased and the local government have ordered this practise to cease!

It is important to ensure that there is minimum time from plucking to the start of withering as in hot countries tea can be spoilt at this stage. It is possible to see if a leaf has been hand plucked or machine harvested by examining the dry leaf as hand plucked leaf will be whole and look like a leaf whereas machine harvested will be a mixture of whole and cut leaf showing serrated edges. Machine harvesting is less selective and done with less care to the leaf but this does not always mean it produces an inferior tea. Green teas then go to the fixing or *kill green* stage missing out the next withering, disruption and oxidation stages.

Withering

The leaves will begin to wilt due to water loss, beginning at the plucking stage, but they are kept to wither for a period of time to further become flaccid. This withering stage is used to remove excess water from the turgid leaves sometimes losing 25-30% water, the *physical wither*, and also to allow important chemical reactions to take place which are the *chemical wither*. Losing water

79

makes the leaf pliable, important in the rolling and bruising stage of the tea process as a rigid leaf would break or crack in the following disruption stage and harm the finished product.

Leaf withering - Image by 仲雄 李 from Pixabay

Green teas are not withered making it important to get these leaves from plucking to the heat treatment stage as quickly as possible with the minimum of leaf damage and minimum oxidation. However, for oxidised black, oolong teas and white tea, withering is a vital step in the tea making process.

Withering is carried out by spreading the leaves on mats on the floor in the open and gently turning them to ensure an even wither. Some teas are withered indoors to control air humidity and draughts whilst other teas, such as puerh teas are usually withered in sunlight giving an effect like sun dried tomatoes. Solar withering may be carried out as UV light plays an important part in some tea flavour development and weather plays a vital part here as wind, air temperature and humidity are factors of importance to a skilled tea processor. Modern controlled methods involve beds of leaves having warm air blown through them with turning airflow to ensure the even wither throughout the batch.

The leaves begin to wilt reducing moisture content from 70-80% to 60-70% causing the cell walls to break down initiating enzymatic oxidation by enzymes, particularly polyphenol oxidase, and creating increaseses in the amounts of flavour chemicals in the leaves. Complex chemicals break down into smaller ones as catechin levels decrease, chlorophyll is reduced by ~15% being converted to pheophytins, the dark pigments important for tea colour formation and reducing the grassy flavour. Proteins, which are no longer required in the dying leaf, break down into amino acids contributing to flavour formation and also caffeine increases from this protein degradation as the amino acids then utilise the nitrogen to make caffeine which, in the soil, will protect the mother plant due to its seed and pest toxicity. Carbohydrates break down into sugars which later react together in the heat treatment process to provide further tea flavour. Lipids, fat molecules, break down into smaller volatile compounds responsible for tea flavours. Fragrances produced by these complex biochemical reactions rise due to higher levels of aromatics, such as geraniol and linalool, which are responsible for the specific fruit aroma in the withering room with the unsaturated fatty acid part of the lipid contributing to the grassy odour of the withering process much the same as when new mown grass smells

If the leaves are withered too long, polyphenol and peroxidase activity will cease due to dehydration. Around 14 hours is the optimum withering period but 20 hours is the maximum before adverse flavour changes occur so often tea is withered overnight. Withering will begin the moment the leaf is separated from the bush so to control the withering period the time taken from picking to the factory is important which is why most tea estates have factories of their own.

Unwithered leaves produce black teas higher in theoflavins but lower in thearubigins resulting in black teas that are bright, brisk but thin, and correspondingly, harder withers produced teas lower in theoflavins but higher in thearubigins, so less brightness and briskness, but improved body.

Bruising (Disruption)

Cell bruising, sometimes called *disruption,* breaks the cell structure allowing contact between polyphenols in the vacuole and enzymes such as the important *polyphenol oxidase* in the cell cytoplasm which together cause enzymatic oxidation to take place in a controlled manner. In the intact plant, the enzymes are not in contact with the polyphenols but disruption ruptures the membrane allowing contact for enzymatic oxidation to take place. The leaves are bruised, torn or macerated, which may be carried out by hand shaking and tossing or tumbling in baskets thereby lightly bruising the leaves on their edges, or more extensive leaf disruption carried out by taking a bunch of leaves and rolling or kneading them on a bamboo table almost like a washboard this being the *orthodox* method. Maceration of the leaf may be also be done by machinery in a rotavane where two plates rotate to mimic the hand rolling with the plate distance and pressure applied largely determining the amount of leaf bruising. It is the amount of bruising that leads to oolong teas which can be from lightly oxidised to heavily oxidised tea. The range of oxidation gives oolongs, partially oxidised teas, a complexity above all other teas with a large range of flavours which some tea drinkers favour. Examination of the dry tea leaf will show browning of light bruising around the edges of the pieces, a characteristic of many oolong teas.

First flush Darjeelings often show brown and green parts of the leaves and, whilst it is described as black tea, it is quite near an oolong type tea. Oolongs have complex flavours created during the complex manufacturing process where the delicate fragrances are not too overpowered by the strong notes characteristic of black teas.Fully oxidised black tea is completely macerated in the *crush, tear, curl (CTC)* method. In this method the leaf is macerated to a pulp of very small pieces that black tea drinkers are familiar with.

Oxidation

Spontaneous oxidation starts slowly in the withering phase and is then accelerated into a more controlled oxidation process after the leaves are bruised. Oxidising is both enzymatic, where enzymes must be present for the reaction to take place, and non-enzymatic which occurs slowly and only requires the presence of oxygen with the chemical substrate. When carried out for oolong and black teas the green leaves turn brown and characteristic flavours are produced, this requiring the skill of a good tea producer to make the best tea from the disruption and oxidation steps.

Polyphenol oxidase, an extremely important enzyme in tea manufacture, changes tea polyphenols (catechins) to *theaflavins,* (flavus means yellow in Latin), orange/yellow compounds which give astringency, briskness, brightness and colour. These in turn react with other catechins to make thearubigins (ruby means red) which contribute to the coppery, chocolate brown colour, mouth feel and body of the tea liquor. These thearubigins further react with sugars and amino acids creating large polymerised (joined up) molecules responsible for tea flavours. This means that a chain of chemical reactions are started by enzymes in the leaf and a jigsaw of chemicals react together to form complicated molecules which contribute to make tea taste and colour. There is a great deal of scientific research currently underway on the withering and oxidation stages to determine how the chemical reactions and oxidation can be maipulated by the control of temperature, humidity and availability of air and even the quality of the light.

The disruption stage will partly determine the extent of oxidation due to the

83

mixing of cell contents. Green tea is not an oxidised tea but even green tea has undergone a small level of oxidation as the process starts when the leaf is plucked. Some damage to the leaf occurs in the picking baskets and even more with machine harvested leaves as they will be cut, so even a 'non-oxidised' tea will have a small amount of oxidisation. No commercial tea is ever 100% oxidised as even black tea in storage will still undergo non-enzymatic oxidation and go stale.

CTC tea is the shortest oxidation time because the cells are smashed to small pieces so a great deal of cell damage has occurred and the particle size is very small compared with a whole leaf giving a large surface area for oxygen availability. Large particle leaf and whole leaf require a skilled tea manager to know when the optimum oxidation has occurred. Many scientific methods have been tested but the basic principal of what is best for the finished tea has always been down to taste by a skilled tea taster. Oxidation stops in the next stage when heat is applied to kill the enzymes.

Fixing / Kill-green

Fixing is done to stop the tea leaf oxidation at a desired level by heating the tea leaves to denature the enzymes thereby deactivating the oxidative enzymes without damaging the flavour of the tea and also removing unwanted odours in the leaves. Fixing occurs in two different stages, the "enzyme kill" stage which deactivates most but not all, and the "final firing" or drying stage, this being done in one step in CTC manufacture. This earlier *kill green* stage, is a high heat, quick process lasting under one minute where the heat is applied by steaming, which is typical for Japanese teas, or by dry heat using pan-frying in a wok, the Chinese craft way, or baking the leaves or "panning" in a rolling drum.

Rolling drum   (Wikipedia images)   Pan frying

These different methods give rise to teas of different characteristics in that steaming keeps the colour very bright, emerald green with fresh vegetal flavours whereas dry heat will toast the leaf a little giving a more olive green appearance and nutty, toasty flavours.

In some white teas, and some black teas, such as CTC blacks, the kill-green is done simultaneously with gentle drying. The heat in this process also reduces the moisture content to ~10-13% an acceptable level for storage.

Sweltering / Yellowing (Yellow tea only)

Unique to yellow teas, an uncommon tea, after fixing warm, moist tea leaves are lightly heated in a closed container, wrapped in paper or deep piled for up to 48 hours causing the green leaves to turn yellow in a process similar to composting. The piling or wrapping reduces the available air/oxygen and crucially allows aromas to be reabsorbed into the tea and the chemical oxidation is very slow after the initial fixing due to reduced availability of air. The resulting leaves produce a beverage that has a distinctive yellowish-green hue due to transformations of the leaf chlorophyll and has a unique taste.

Shaping

The shape of the "made" tea is given to the leaf and can be carried out at, or after, the kill green stage. They may be gently rolled or, wiry or tightly rolled pellets, Long Jing (Dragonwell) tea leaves are pressed against the sides of the wok and are characteristically flat shaped, whereas some oolongs are rolled into a tight ball and Japanese Senchas are rolled and twisted producing characteristic needle like leaves. The more tightly rolled the leaves, the longer they will retain their freshness. Some Jasmine tea are called pearls due to being rolled into the shape of a pearl and this tight rolling keepes the delicate flavour in the tea.

Drying

The later stage, "final firing", is done by baking the leaves for about 20-60 minutes to reduce the water content in the leaves to 3-5% to ensure a stable product for storage and fully denature any remaining enzymes. However, heat during this step results in an initial rise in enzymatic activity as the leaves warm up and 10-15% of theaflavins can be formed in the first 10 minutes as not all the enzymes have been denatured.

Some tea flavours come from this heat process of drying through the maillard reaction which is a chemical reaction between sugars and amino acids. Oolongs may also be baked over charcoal as a final drying and baking stage thereby enhancing the roasting type flavours.

Sorting

The above processes have made unrefined tea leaving one more stage to sort the tea leaves to make a good finished product. This unrefined, unfinished tea is called *maocha* in China, although this term is usually used for unfinished Puerh tea because much of the unrefined tea is sorted before leaving the factory. Unrefined tea in Japan is called *aracha* where factory tea is usually collected together and blended after factory processing. Unfinished tea contains oversize and other not properly processed leaves, leaves from other plants that have fallen into the harvest, twigs, insects and any other matter that needs sorting out.

Grading

At the last process of making black tea, leaves are separated according to the particle size using sieves, and then tea is cleaned by removing the dust. This process is called grading. Grading is physical on particle size rather than grading tea by cup quality.

Before going any further, many tea drinkers are familiar with the term *orange pekoe* which the tea industry uses to describe a basic, medium-grade black tea consisting of many whole tea leaves of a specific size. However, the term is sometimes used as a marketing description of any generic black tea and sometimes the word is used to make the consumer believe erroneously that it is a specific variety of black tea. The origin of the word "pekoe" may be derived from the transliterated mispronunciation of the Amoy (Xiamen) dialect word for a Chinese tea known as "white down/hair" *pèh-ho or* from the Chinese "white flower" *pèh-hoe.* This means that it is correctly pronounced *peck-ho* not *peek-ho.* Sir Thomas Lipton, the 19th-century British grocer magnate is credited with popularizing the term "orange pekoe" as a marketing ploy but the 'orange' has no relevence at all to the tea flavour. There are two explanations, though neither is definitive and neither has much use to the average tea drinker where it is a meaningless term.

- The Dutch East India Company played a central role in bringing tea to Europe and may have marketed the tea as "orange" to suggest association with the Dutch House of Orange.

- The copper colour of a high-quality, oxidized leaf before drying, or the final bright orange colour of the dried leaf in the finished tea may be related to the name. The orange colour of bud and one leaf appears when the tea is fully oxidized.

Flavouring

Tea is very susceptible to picking up odours from anything near with a distinctive odour which is why care is needed when storing tea. Common and traditional flavoured teas are jasmine, osmanthus and rose but there is a great deal of confusion between a scented tea and a herbal infusion made without tea which those marketing tea do not make very clear. The ingredient list on the label will indicate whether the packet contains tea or not.

It is worth explaining jasmine tea, in particular, which is a common green flavoured tea often served in Chinese restaurants as "Chinese Tea". Jasmine is a good tea flavour as one of the flavour chemicals in tea is *jasmonate*. Chinese restaurants serve the customers what they think we want but Jasmine tea is just one of many teas that goes under the banner of 'Chinese tea'. The lower quality jasmine teas have visual jasmine flowers in the finished tea as the tea producers would like the consumer to think that this is a sign of quality – **it is not**, it is quite the reverse as the lower grade teas still have the jasmine petals left in the finished tea! The best jasmine teas are made by taking made tea and spreading it over a layer of jasmine flowers or mixing them in. The jasmine flowers should be buds that open in the tea pile immediately releasing their flavour into the tea overnight and sometimes tea workers describe hearing a popping noise as the buds open releasing their fresh scent to the tea. The flowers are renewed with fresh flowers, this repeated 3-5 times, then every flower must be removed, as these are bitter, and the tea then left to dry which is obviously extremely labour intensive. Pearl jasmine tea is rolled into a tight ball thereby locking in the jasmine flavour and it is delicious.

Fermenting

These are black teas *(heicha)* in China which are aged by a further microbial fermentation to make black tea such as puerh, which is largely unfamiliar, but gaining popularity in the west. It is a true microbial process similar to making blue cheese from the basic Cheddar type cheeses in that the original, and the most authentic process, relies on natural flora from the leaves and plantations being a very slow maturation process but modern science has hastened this process by controlling the microbial changes leading to product which, on a like for like basis, will never quite match the natural process. This is a tea that some tea drinkers favour almost to the exclusion of other teas as there is such a vast range of flavours. The fact that microbes are involved makes this tea the only truly fermented tea rather than the widely misquoted oxidised teas, whih are often erroneously referred to as fermented teas. The slow maturation of the process can take several years and like a fine wine command fantastic prices.

Fermented teas are often compressed and wrapped and displayed like plates are displayed in the west. See Page 101.

Puerh tea example commercially available

CHAPTER EIGHT

TEA CATEGORIES

Tea leaves are processed as above to produce thousands of different flavoured and coloured teas so, to put some order into this, they are grouped into categories according to production methods each having a characteristic flavour profile. These categories are a little artificial like colours in a rainbow but there are definite bands favoured by each tea drinker who will favour one category of tea above others which can then be further explored within that group. Many people brought up on black tea say they do not like green tea having only tried a low grade tea bag of poor quality tea where the preparation has been poor in that the water has been too hot or the tea has been oversteeped. Appreciating all the categories of tea by understanding the differences and how to correctly prepare the tea will open up a new world of tea flavours.

What this actually means is that all categories of tea can theoretically be made from the leaves of one type of bush of Camellia sinensis using different production techniques but this never happens as this disregards cultivar, terroir and skill for the many different teas below. The categories are:-

- **White tea (baicha)**
- **Yellow tea (huangcha)**
- **Green tea (lucha)**
- **Blue tea (wulongcha – *Wulong* is the modern Pinyin spelling**
- **Black tea (Hongcha- called red tea in China)**
- **Puerh tea (heicha- Black tea)**

White Tea

White tea can be made from all tea bushes and is the least processed of all tea. It is basically plucked and withered for ~72 hours preferably in sunlight and may be gently dried at low temperatures ~65°C so the choice of cultivar is key to the best teas as this is where the taste character starts. There is no generally accepted definition of white tea so we have the usual confusion over tea nomenclature of whether a tea is authentic as defined by one or more cultivars, processing method, region, or whether the tea name refers to a tea style making this excellent category of tea difficult to pin down. Currently on sale as white tea are teas that meet the following criteria:-

1. Hand picked from unopened buds, which are silvery white and covered in fine hairs. The downy immature bud, or sometimes the bud and one leaf, are harvested before the leaf has developed too much chlorophyll and sometimes before the sun has fully risen in the day with some white teas being described as *"moonlight"* tea as the leaves are picked before dawn and the sun has had chance to turn the buds green, and early in the year at the very start of spring between mid March and mid April

2. As above but may contain bud and one leaf having a greener quality and a stronger flavour.

3. The plucking standards as above but only using a white cultivar such as Da Bai (Big white) which has light green leaves. In China, white tea is largely defined by the plant from which it is derived, e.g. Camellia sinensis var. zhenge bai hao or var. fuding bai hao.

4. In India, white tea is made from any cultivar, such as AV2, with minimal leaf processing and the white refering to the liquor colour.

Indian processors are sun drying small leaf tea and calling it "white tea" and due to the terroir the flavour profile is quite different to Chinese white tea. However, Puer tea leaves are also minimally processed, dried in the sun and then compressed but is not considered white tea as puerh tea is usually defined as black tea

5. There is a Taiwanese tea cultivar called Anji Bai Cha (Anji white tea) made from a light green cultivar discovered in the early 1980s that has a yellow tinge in the unprocessed leaves but is still considered a green not a white tea.

The Tea Association of the USA has proposed a new definition for White Tea.

1. Produced in accordance with the strict harvesting and processing guidelines as originally established and followed in the Fujian province of China.

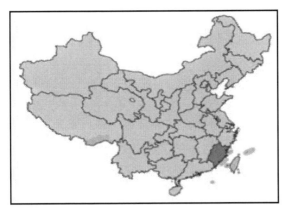

Wkipedia - Fujian Province

2. Only the hand-picked, unopened leaf bud, or the hand-picked, unopened leaf bud and first two leaves from the first seasonal flush of the

92

Camellia sinensis plant should be harvested. The raw tea leaf should not be rolled or otherwise have its leaf/cellular structure ruptured.

3. Tea leaves may be dried and/or be steamed (or similar enzyme de-activation) and then dried. The finished tea should be packaged in such a way as to protect the physical and organoleptic quality of the tea that contributes to the uniqueness of this form.

4. White Tea can be made by any tea producing country providing manufacture conforms to the above harvesting and processing steps. (i.e, minimal processing).

The only agreement, if that is the correct term, seems to be that white tea is plucked as unopened bud, or bud and one leaf, not necessarily a white tea cultivar, and withered for up to ~72 hours with or without UVB rayed sunlight then very gently fired to dry the tea and stop further oxidation making claims that white tea is not oxidised incorrect. Note, the tea is lightly oxidised from the solar withering, but not bruised, so enzymatic oxidation is minimised. The emphasis is on the solar withering which is the important step in white tea manufacture as the UV light acts on the polyphenols and carotenoids to develop the fragrant floral notes of this tea. All these methods are used for white tea so *original* is probably better to use than *authentic* but some non-original white teas are authentic and wonderful. The traditional, original standard is that true white tea can only be made from the unopened bud, or bud and two leaves, from Da Bai Hao bushes picked early season, preferably early in the day and preferably solar withered.

White tea has high levels of volatiles, especially hexenal and hexanol which have a green grassy odour and have wonderful flowery aroma.

Yellow Tea

Yellow tea is a rather scarce tea and good yellow tea is not only hard to come by but is very expensive. There are hundreds of of green teas but there are only three true kinds of yellow tea Meng Ding Huang Ya, Huoshan Huang Ya (from Annhui province), and Junshan Yinzhen (from Hunan province). The process for making yellow tea is similar to that of green with an extra unique additional step called *men huan*, or "sealing yellow". After the fixing stage, kill green, the tea is encased or smothered in thick paper or cloth, Junshan Yin Shen being stored in a wooden box to reduce air and oxidation, so the tea is allowed to oxidize at a slower rate to produce a softer taste than is found in most green teas and also giving the leaves a slightly yellow colouring during the drying process. At intervals the tea is fried again and re-wrapped to cool to oxidize slightly. This process continues for up to three days and then slow roasted at the finish, making this a lengthy expensive process. Making yellow tea removes the characteristic grassy smell and astringency of green tea.

Green Tea

Green teas are made by leaving the leaves to wither and then firing them to prevent oxidation so Green teas are an unoxidised tea. The leaves are wilted in shallow layers for 8-14 hours then heated to inactivate the enzymes to prevent polyphenols from being oxidised so contain a high level of polyphenols and little of the highly coloured oxidative compounds. There are two kinds of green tea determined by the enzyme deactivation stage these being *steamed* green tea, largely made in Japan, and dry heat *air/ pan-fired* tea largely made in China, although both types are made in both countries. Steaming tends to keep the emerald green colour whereas pan firing tends to turn the tea leaves olive green and contribute to a fired, biscuity taste. Additionally, with green tea, whether the leaves have been shaded prior to harvest is important to the final flavour as shading will stop sunlight acting on the plant's chloropyhyll creating the energy to produce caffeine from amino acids making shaded tea richer in amino acids so more umami flavour. Green tea does not age well in storage as non-enzymatic oxidation can still continue and spoil the tea and the consequent short shelf life is one of the reasons oxidised teas became so widespread. Green tea colour comes from chlorophyll and the ratio of chlorophyll A, dark green, and chlorophyll B, yellowish green and from water soluble flavonols, yellow. When steeped green tea is left standing it becomes darker due to pheophytin and pheophorbide which are the breakdown products of chlorophyll.

Green tea amounts to ~20% of the total world consumption primarily in Asian countries, China and Japan and there really are thousands, of green teas available. For many Europeans black tea with milk, is the drink of choice and for many the only association with green tea is the occassional attempt at dipping a low grade teabag in a mug of hot water but, with the range of green teas available, the point is missed about this type of tea – never taken with milk. Skilful tea crafting produces an unlimited number of green teas typically made from sinensis. Sinensis has small leaf and a more delicate floral flavour whereas assamica produces a more robust, fuller flavour tea.

Low grade tea in a teabag is not a good way to be introduced to the delights of the complex flavours green tea has to offer. When sampling green teas it is essential to know the process and whether the tea is baked or steam fixed, and whether the leaves have been in full sun or shaded bushes. Notwithstanding the fixing and shading differences there are many cultivars, terroirs, the growing methods, plucking standards and every step of the process, including the cup infusing, which can be controlled to give different flavour balance. It seems that to arrive at the final flavour there are so many variables that making the same tea twice is almost impossible.

Oolong (Wulong) Tea

Oolong (Black Dragon Tea) which in Chinese is called Qing cha (Clear Tea), is a category of tea that is ~20-80% oxidised creating a wide flavour variability and they may be further roasted or baked over charcoal which further increases their variability. Oolong tea, because it is a bruised tea, will be partly oxidised somewhere between ~30-40% for light oolongs and 50-70% for dark oolongs. These are teas that have a floral aroma made by withering followed by shaking the leaf or rolling to bruise the edges, drying and sometimes further high temperature baking to fully dry and deliver the final flavour profile. Partial controlled oxidation is achieved by bruising the leaves with the amount of bruising determining the amount of enzymatic oxidation the leaf undergoes. Hand processed oolongs are made by taking handfuls of withered leaf and kneading them on bamboo like a washboard. The juices in the bruised parts of the leaves undergo enzymatic oxidation making oolongs somewhere between a green and black tea with large colour variation and wide range of delicate flavours so oolongs are a very complex and varied category of tea. Some of the lighter oolongs resemble green tea but the leaf edges will show light brown fringes where the leaf is bruised on the olive green leaf, whereas heavily oxidised leaves will resemble a fully oxidised leaf.

Ball oolongs, usually the higher quality oolongs, are made by repeatedly wrapping the leaves in cloth extremely tightly into a ball then rolling the ball to squash and bruise the leaves which exude juices. The leaves are then removed from the cloth, the leaf ball broken open and the leaves put through a flash dryer, this step being repeated several times to make a very complex tea flavour due to non-enzymatic oxidation. The flavour of oolongs is readily available due to some of the juices being dried on the outside of the leaf thereby releasing the fragrant notes quickly when steeped, so a short infusion is recommended to release and retain the floral notes. The leaves are shaped by rolling them into long curly leaves like Da Hong Pao or pressed and rolled into tea pearls like the Dong Ding, Gunpowder, and Ti Guan Yin. This requires a great deal of skill to give a consistent tea that is very labour intensive but will give some of the finest oolongs.

There is often an extra step in oolong manufacture of baking where the tea is baked at high temperature which introduces a nutty, roasted flavour. This baking, like the range of oxidation, is varied and can be a short, medium or long bake depending on the tea the manufacturer wants, so oolongs can be quite green to dark brown both from the oxidation and baking stages and some tea drinkers will drink nothing but oolongs for the complexity of the flavours they produce.

Black (Red) Tea

The Western term 'black tea' refers to the colour of the oxidized leaves but the Chinese call this Hong Cha (red tea) because of the colour of the tea and for many people this is the only tea they have tried being 78% of the total amount of tea consumed. It should be stated here that black tea is not fermented it is oxidised both by enzymatic oxidation, brought about largely by polyphenol oxidase acting on polyphenols, and non-enzymatic oxidation from chemicals reacting with atmospheric oxygen in the same way that iron rusts. Oolong teas undergo partial enzymatic oxidation and black teas a more complete oxidation, nevertheless, black tea can still be non-enzymatically oxidise during storage causing flavour deterioration. Black teas are made by withering, rolling, oxidising and drying with characteristic darker flavours and colours created during the oxidising and drying stages. The brown colouration comes from oxidised polyphenols which produce thearubigins and theaflavins so black tea will contain less catechins than green tea.

Black tea is typically made from C. assamica, the large-leaved variety, but this is general as both black and green tea can be made from either variety. Black tea flavour is stronger, bolder and more robust than green tea as large leaf C.assamica is the usual variety. A steeped black tea can range in colour from amber to dark brown and the flavour profile can range from bitter, astringent to sweet depending on the oxidation stage and how it was heat processed. Black tea typically has more astringency and bitterness than green tea, but if infused correctly it should be smooth and flavourful. Green tea usually loses its flavour within a year due to atmospheric oxidation spoilage but black tea can retain its flavour for several years due to the more complete oxidation. For this reason, black tea became an important article of trade in China historically as it can withstand long journey times. Originally, green tea was brought to Europe but black tea took centre stage partly due to the stability on the long journey from China. The flavours of single-origin black teas can be broadly described based on where they are from. Different tea origins produce different black tea flavour profiles due to their unique terroir:-

- **Assam tea: bold, malty, brisk**
- **Darjeeling tea: delicate, fruity, floral, light**
- **Nilgiri tea: fragrant, floral**
- **Ceylon black tea: varies by origin, but is generally bold, strong and rich, sometimes with notes of chocolate or spice**
- **Keemun black tea: wine-like, fruity, floral, piney, tobacco-like**
- **Yunnan black tea: chocolate, dark, malty, with notes of spice**
- **Kenyan black tea: bold, astringent, dark**

With some black teas the leaves are left whole (orthodox) or cut into smaller pieces (non-orthodox/CTC) for packaging. To achieve a consistent commercial product CTC teas are often blended to produce a tea with a standard flavour. CTC teas at the leaf disruption stage are macerated into very small particle size to maximise the oxidation process, so no subtlety there.

Black tea grading started with teas from India and is largely leaf quality grading and not necessarily anything directly to do with the cup quality:-

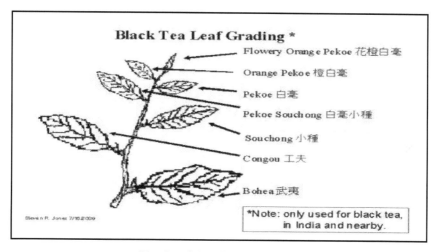

Tea Leaf Grading – Wikipedia

The following grades are used for black tea:-

- **1. Whole leaf**
- **2. Broken leaf**
- **3. Fannings**
- **4. Dust**

These are not an indication of the final cup quality but are leaf grades, nevertheless, generally the more letters the better the tea, examples are as follows :-

- **OP**—Orange Pekoe: main grade, consisting of long wiry leaf without tips
- **FOP**—Flowery Orange Pekoe: high-quality tea with a long leaf and few tips
- **GFOP**—Golden Flowery Orange Pekoe: higher proportion of tip than FOP.
- **TGFOP**—Tippy Golden Flowery Orange Pekoe: the highest proportion of tip,
- **FTGFOP**—Finest Tippy Golden Flowery Orange Pekoe: highest quality grade
- **FTGFOP1 or STGFOP or SFTGFOP**— Special Finest Tippy Golden Flowery Orange Pekoe limited to only the highest quality leaves in the FTGFOP classification

In addition to these above are the broken grades with a 'B' in the classification as in GFBOP (Golden Flowery Broken Orange Pekoe). Smaller particle pekoes are fannings, and there is also tea dust – dust being a particle size not a detrimental term. These grades are physical, not cup quality, and being smaller are found in tea bags. Breaking open a commercial teabag will reveal whether it is small leaf particles (unusual but getting more common), fannings (very small pieces), or dust but it would be unusual to find a high grade tea in either of these two categories. Tea grade is important in determining the amount of tea required to make a good cup, the larger the leaf, the more tea needed and furthermore it will have an impact on infusion time. The larger the leaf, the smaller the surface area exposed to the water and the longer it will take to infuse.

Fermented Tea Black Tea(Puerh/Heicha)

Sometimes referred to as black tea (Hei cha), is a fermented tea produced in Yunnan province, China and is highly prized. Puerh is the most famous and easily procured but other regions now make this fermented tea. but the original, and authentic puerh, will come from Yunnan, in particular the city of Puerh (formerly Simao) and is commonly known as Puerh tea made from large leaves picked as one bud and 3-4 leaves and sometimes from Camellia Taliensis, a large leaf variety closer to the Indian assamica variety. Note, that this is not Camellia sinensis but an ancient relative, possibly a precurser to C. Sinensis, and has a wild, varied genetic content that may harbour useful genes for the tea plant C. Sinensis. C. Taliensis is somewhere between a wild tree and a cultivated tree so is a reasonable example of a 'tea tree in transition'. In 2008, the Chinese government declared puerh tea as a "product with geographical indications" which would restrict the naming of tea as 'Puerh' to tea produced within specific regions of the Yunnan province. Other regions also make dark tea (hei cha) and a less well known basket, uncompressed fermented tea called 'Liu Bao' which is produced in Guangxi province west of Guangdong.

Puerh tea leaves come from trees as listed below usually with decreasing cost down the list:-

- **Wild trees** (Gushu cha – Ancient tea). This is arguably the most sought after being unique in source and flavour and due to the nature of harvesting the leaves will be organic so free of fertilisers or insecticides. The unique flavour profile is often ascribed to the ancient roots going much deeper than young trees so the rich source of minerals is accessed and coupled with the old trees fertilising the immediate ground with mineral rich leaves. The flavour is often described as high on 'minerality' but how signifcant are the deeper roots in accessing soil minerals but see Chapter 5 for a more scientific and credible explanation.

- **Wild arbour** (Shengtai cha yuan) – literally, 'ancient tea groves' are trees, or randomly planted trees from seed that have reverted to feral trees. The ancient ethnic tribes in the Yunnan province often moved due to wars and political changes leaving ancient plantations to go wild. Rediscovered, these trees make unique teas and are also usually organic.

- **Plantation bushes** ('Taidi Cha Yuen' - terrace tea plantation) are considered less prized to those above due to the bushes being densely planted and having the same genetic traits but this is a generality as some superb teas come from plantation trees. Insecticides and fertilisers are often used so can not be marketed as organic products.

Key to this truly fermented tea are bacterial and fungal cultures consisting of multiple strains of aspergillus, penicillium, yeasts and an assortment of other microflora found on the leaves and in the fermenting piles varying widely throughout Yunnan. The processes can be compared to original blue cheese manufacture which relies on the natural flora of the cave and takes at least a long time to mature in flavour but can improve like a good wine over 20 years, or quickly processed like an inexpensive Danish Blue cheese where the tea matures in a matter of months. Over time, puerh acquires an earthy flavour due to the mould formation.

Historically, this tea came about by the time taken to trade tea long distances over difficult terrain such as along the Tea Horse Road in China. Green tea quality would deteriorate, having a short shelf life when exposed to air, particularly if it became moist so the time taken to cover the long distances was overcome by compressing the tea into cakes saving space and reducing air spoilage. In so doing, the moisture trapped in the compressed cakes allowed mould to form and this mould eventually became an accepted and expected flavour of this tea. To make Puerh the leaves are withered, heated to fix the green, sun dried, and hand sorted. Following this the leaves are put in a cylinder with holes in the bottom and steam applied so the leaves sink down into the cylinder. A cloth bag is then placed over the cylinder and inverted to put the tea in the bag, the top of the bag screwed up and put into a mould press or a large stone weight is rolled around to squash the tea and to fully compress it to form a disc with a small indentation where the screwed top of the bag went. The moisture in the disc allows the fermentation to take place so these teas age like old wines and develop flavours over many years. Due to compression the fermentation on the outside of the block can ferment aerobically, in the presence of air, but will ferment anaerobically on the inside of the block where oxygen is reduced. This will give a range of flavours throughout the block and a complexity to the cup. The common shapes of the blocks to be found on the market are as follows:-

- **Zhuan (Juan) Cha (Brick Tea)**
- **Bing (Beeng) Cha (Cake Tea)**
- **Toa (Tua) Cha (Bell/Bird's nest Shape)**
- **Jin Cha (Mushroom)**
- **Long Zhu (Dragon Pearl, usually small)**
- **Jingua Cha - Melon Tea**

Zhuan (Juan) Cha -Brick Tea

Bing (Beeng) Cha - Cake Tea

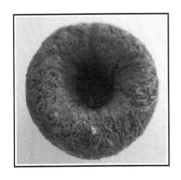

Tua Cha - Bird's nest

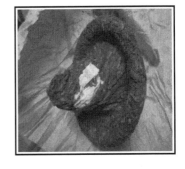

Jin Cha (Mushroom)

Long Zhu -Dragon Pearl

Jingua Cha - Melon Tea

Puerh tea shapes – Wikipedia

Flow Diagram for Tea Manufacture

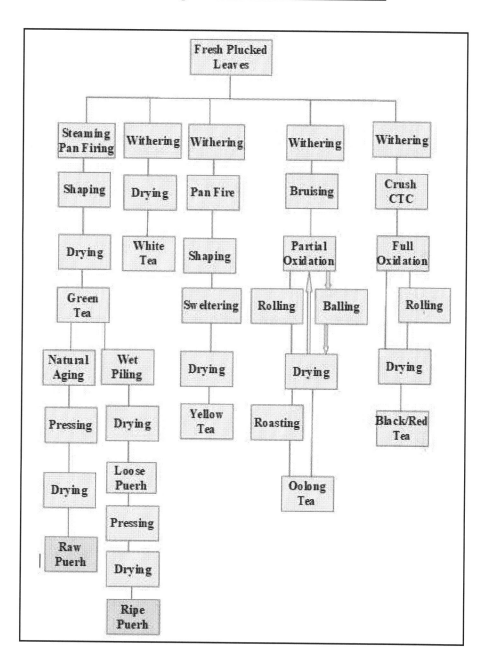

CHAPTER NINE

SIGNATURE TEAS

Do not take tea tasting too seriously as only professionals should do this, for the great majority tea can be an exciting adventure. Japan has a word which may be appropriate, it is *Chajin*, literally meaning "tea person" or "tea lover" not necessarily being a tea professional. Signature teas to be tried are recommended below which illustrate ththe range of each category with an explanation about the teas and help with the unfamiliar names. Big business works hard to produce a consistent product, which is admirable, but this is what some tea adventurers may not necessarily want or expect.

Searching for that perfect tea has a three dimensional approach:-

1. Try teas from each of the "categories of tea" (white, oolong, green etc.) to identify your preferred category. Some people drink green, some black others oolongs, and become quite proficient at identifying the characteristics to look for in a particular category, so try a few examples of each category of tea.

2. Taste different tea styles from the category of tea you like. For example oxidised teas could be malty, chocolate, strong flavoured Assams or delicate flowery muscatel Darjeelings so try different types of black teas, Assams, Darjeelings, Chinese Keemun, Ceylon.

3. Taste different teas from within that style, for example, Darjeeling oxidised teas from different estates, Goomtee, Margaret's Hope, Castleton, different seasons/flushes, spring, summer and autumn and different elevations which is very important with Ceylon teas.

106

To summarise, firstly, find a category of tea that you particularly enjoy, then find your preferred taste profile style within that category and then explore different taste profiles within the tea you most prefer. Whatever age you are, that should take you the rest of your life! Small packages, up to ~50grams, are recommended to keep the cost down and the tea fresh as some teas can lose their charm when exposed to air. Some suppliers offer 10g sample selection packs of particular genres of teas being an excellent way of quickly and inexpensively comparing a number of different teas, and other suppliers have 'tea clubs' where monthly samples of different teas to try are sent out each month with a little explanation about the tea, the best way to steep the tea and tasting notes.

There are so many teas to try that the choice can be overwhelming, so to help understand the range of flavours possible some comparison teas have been selected showing the wide range available. A favourite tea can be found, and that particular tea can be further investigated. To illustrate tea flavour ranges within a group two very different, but typical, teas within a category have been selected and the journey can begin. Below are the recommended teas to demonstrate the range of tea complexity being teas which have become popular over the years. Firstly, try an inexpensive tea sample from the signature teas below from a reputable supplier to understand the taste that can be delivered, then, as tea knowledge developes, try more expensive and confirmed genuine teas.

White Tea

It was believed that white tea was discovered during the Song Dynasty (920-1269), however, earlier references to white tea have been traced as far back as the Tang Dynasty (618-907). White tea was a favourite of Emperor Huizong (reigned 1100-1126), a tea connoisseur who first mentioned it in his book called

"Da Guan Cha Lun" (A Treatise on Tea) about a tea plant with jade white leaves which was probably a pale green tea. Over the next several centuries, powdered white tea and the Song Tea Ceremony were abandoned for loose-leaf tea and white tea was lost. In 1885, select varieties of the tea plant were developed for white tea when a new white variety was discovered in Fuding. In 1982 a single white tea bush, now known as the Ancestor of Bai Cha, was found in An Ji County, Zhejiang province, China, which is believed to be the tea plant mentioned in the book above. White tribute tea for the emporer was once plucked by virgins with gloved hands who snipped the tea leaves with golden scissors to present the Emperor with a tea of complete purity. Mariage Freres, a top class French Tea House, sell a virgin white tea today and the company claim women wearing fine gloves collect the sole pekoe, or bud, of the imperial harvest with gold scissors, taking care not to harm the shoots. (No mention of the other requirement for the ladies!). A single pot of this tea will set you back £25 in a private club in Manchester, England. Sacred White is also available direct from Mariage Freres for around £58 for four 5g envelopes – though it does come in a porcelain caddy!

China has a legend that a girl called Langu discovered the original Da Bai Hao bush on Tai Mu mountain in Fuding, Fujian. She used the tea from this plant to cure disease and the tea at that time was called Lu Xue Cha, which means green tea from immortals. Another legend involves a man named Chen Minghuan who was led to the bush by a vision of the Tai Mu Niang Niang. There is an interesting similarity to this myth and the myth about the origins of Tie Guan Yin in Southern Fujian. The Guan Yin goddess is famous for relieving suffering both from disease and poverty.

Original white tea comes from Fuding and Zhenghe counties in Fujian province but excellent white teas are now produced in other regions including

India using the clonal tea AV2 and the taste is deliciously fragrant and long lasting making a taste comparison with Fuding tea an enjoyable experience. White tea has no agreed definition but is well worth trying the different styles. The Fujian province Zheng He tea bush can be very large, from three to 5 meters high and the buds are smaller than the Fuding Da Bai and have leaves that are yellowish green. This bush produces buds later in the spring and can be processed as green tea, black tea, as well as white tea made from this bush. The Fuding Da Bai bush produces bigger, fatter, longer buds that are thick with hair. In Fuding the four grades of tea in order of perceived quality are as follows but it must be pointed out that 4th grade can still be delicious!

- 1st Grade - Bai Hao Yin Zhen (Silver Needles)
- 2nd Grade - Bai Mu Dan
- 3rd Grade - Gong Mei
- 4th grade - Shou Mei

Three white teas are recommended to try because they are all so different:-

Bai Hao Yin Zhen (White Hair Silver Needle)

Bai Hao Yin Zhen (White Hair Silver Needle), 'bud tea' made from the unopened buds of the Fuding or Zhenghe Da Bai cultivars from the Fujian province of China, is one of the finest quality white teas and a must to try. The lyoung leaf buds are covered with white, downy hairs from where it gets its name as they look like needles in the cup having very little green chlorophyll so have a silvery appearance. Zhenge is usually darker, with a longer piled time for oxidation than Fuding, yielding a tea with fuller body.The difficulty of Yin Zhen tea is that the buds, and only buds, must be hand picked early on a day without rain or too much mist, and before the sun increases the level of chlorophyll, so the yield of this tea is very small and the tea expensive.

Bai Mu Dan (White Peony)

Bai Mu Dan (White Peony) is also made from *Da Bai* (Large White) cultivars and includes new leaves as well as the bud, and has come about because of the greater yield due to plucking the top two newly developed leaves. It is considered a lesser grade than Yin Zhen but has a fuller flavour.

Shou Mei (Long Noble Life Eyebrow)

Shou Mei (Long Noble Life Eyebrow) is an aged white tea often purchased as a compressed cake like puerh tea so ageing will improve this tea. In Fuding, they have a saying: **One year tea, three years medicine, seven years treasure**, meaning in one year it is just tea, in three years it has developed health benefits but after seven years it has come of age and is prized by tea connoisseurs. It is a grade down from bai mu dan due to the later picking.

Green Tea

To appreciate green tea it is very important to infuse correctly due to the bitter catechins which are extracted very quickly so the art of infusing this tea is to not boil the water and not to oversteep. Infusion guides for the teas are given later in tea preparation. Two teas have been selected which are vastly different; **Long Jing (Dragonwell)** which is Chinese roasted or wok fried tea, and **Sencha** which is a Japanese steam fixed tea, both being typical of the country of origin. The recommendation is to buy an example tea and explore within the preferred tea. Summarising the general difference between a typical Chinese tea and a typical Japanese tea is as follows:-

- Cultivar used to make the tea, often Yabukita in Japan, more cultivar variation in China.

- The bushes may be shaded prior to harvest – mainly Japan but usually not standard sencha.

- Enzyme deactivation is by steaming (Japan), dry heat (China).

- Blending of producers is almost universal in Japan so more consistency in Japanese greens which gives a reliability and uniformity to the tea but not necessarily the excitement of discovering a unique tea.

- Variability greater in China which produces more hand made tea. Japanese tea is usually mechanically produced (unless you pay a hefty price) so is more standardised.

- Elevation for Japanese tea growing is lower compared with many China teas.

Long Jing (Dragon Well)

Typical flattened spear shaped Long Jing tea leaves

Long Jing (Dragon Well) tea has been one of the most famous teas in China for a long time and is a classic representation of wok-roasted green tea.

Authentic, original Long Jing, is produced in Long Jing Village situated at the shore of Xi Hu (West Lake) near Hangzhou in Zhejiang province in China, the most famous being called Shi Feng (Lion Peak) Long Jing Xi Hu has a mild climate with rain and fog all year round with little sun creating natural shady conditions which help the tea leaves retain more theanine.

Long Jing was granted the status of Gong Cha, or Imperial Tea, in the Qing dynasty by the Kangxi Emperor (1654–1722). Legend has it that his grandson, the Emperor Qianlong (1711–1799), visited West Lake and was presented with a cup of Long Jing tea at the Hu Gong Temple under the Lion Peak Mountain (Shi Feng Shan). In front of the Hu Gong Temple were 18 tea bushes on which he later conferred special imperial status. The legend says that he saw some ladies picking the tea at the foot of the mountain and being so interested in their movements he decided to pick some (the legend fails to say whether it was the ladies or the tea that attracted him – we assume it was the tea!) but while picking the tea he received news of his mother's illness. He put the leaves in his sleeve and left Hangzhou to visit his mother, the Empress Dowager, in Beijing. She smelt the fragrance of the leaves from his sleeves so Qianlong ordered this tea to be brewed for her. She revived and praised the tea as a remedy for all ills and from then on Shi Feng Longjing tea has been listed as a tribute tea. The original trees are still living and the tea they produced was very expensive but produced with due care to the highest standards commanding very high prices but recently plucking has stopped to preserve these living legends. There are many Long Jing style teas available, perhaps not truly authentic, but still teas of good quality and there is so much variation in this tea that even when a special Long Jing has been found it may be different the following year. Most Dragon Well on the market is made from a commercial cultivar known as Long Jing #43 or Wu Niu Zao (Black Buffalo Early), both varieties meaning it cannot be from the 18 original Long Jing trees which would be random, cross bred, sexually propagated mixed varieties. Long Jing #43 consistently flushes early so can command a high early tea price (ming qian) but possibly may lose some of the originality of older type bushes which are now more highly prized.

The roasting is done by hand in iron pans, the roasters using their bare hands to press the leaves on the side of the wok to better experience the heat and understand the development of the tea leaves, a process that can take up to five years to properly master. The tea is also pressed between paper to produce characteristic spear-like flattened leaves.

There are hundreds of Long Jing producers just within the Xihu area so consideration needs to be given to terroir, tea-making mastery, harvesting season, quality, notwithstanding the issue of mislabelling. In July 2011, Hangzhou's West Lake district's Long Jing Tea Industry Association received a geographical indications trademark for Long Jing tea as an anti-counterfeiting measure which means other regions cannot use the brand name 'West Lake (Xi Hu) Long Jing' to promote their teas so Xi Hu tea must be grown within a designated 168 square kilometre area. A quick internet search of a genuine premium Long Jing spring tea costs $100/100g, an acceptable Long Jing tea costs £15/100g but if the taste justifies the price, it is fair. For example, in 2015 the first batch of pre-Guyu Long Jing tea, picked on April 7 2015, sold for 2,000 yuan (£250) per kilo, later batches were selling for around 300 yuan (£38) per kilo with the fall in price mainly due to the buying of luxury goods being frowned on in China. Pre-Qingming is the lightest, for the refined palate of tea experts, while pre-Guyu tea is a little stronger, but still very good. Work your way up the taste ladder and cost and be a brave chajin!

Shi Feng (Lion Peak) is the most highly prized of the West Lake varieties being the original growing area and, due to the elevation, can be the best of West Lake Long Jing tea. It is also the most expensive of all due to quality, reputation, provenance, rarity, demand – it has them all - but if you want a treat then dig deep into your pocket and try this gold standard Chinese tea.

Mei Jia Wu variety of West Lake Long Jing tea is famous for its jade green colour produced in Mei Jian Wu village as a high quality green tea .

Xi Hu Long Jing tea is a general name for tea from this area so includes the tea plantations of all the villages in this region. Xi Hu tea must be grown within a designated 168 square kilometre area.

Qian Tang Long Jing tea is also produced in the Zhejiang province but just outside the West Lake area so is not as expensive and many consider it not to be a true Long Jing but usually it makes good tea.

Most Long Jing for Europe is exported through Zhejiang Tea Corporation, which collects tea from all over Zhejiang and beyond and is blended together so whilst the varieties above are important many fine Long Jing teas are available for very reasonable prices.

Sencha

Typical neeedle like Sencha leaves

114

Sencha is Japanese green tea (*ryokucha*) representing ~80% of all the green tea sold in Japan. The *Yabukita* cultivar is the most popular in Japan used for 75% of Japanese tea and 90% in Shizuoka prefecture, where it was developed and helped Japan make good tasting tea, with a high yielding plant and, most important in Japan, resistant to frost. It is also the consistency of this cultivar which is beneficial to Japanese tea with a culture of tight quality control over the whole process. This is one major difference between Japanese and Chinese green teas where the tight quality control, uniform cultivar and final blending produce a uniform product that the buyer can rely on. Chinese tea, being more artisanal tea, beomes a more varied product but some would argue that is the fun of tea. So if you enjoy tea exploration Chinese teas are for you but if you want reliability from your favoured tea you will not better Japanese teas.

In Japan the flushes are called *shincha* or ichibancha (first), *nibancha* (second), *sanbancha* (third) and *yonbancha* (fourth). The term shincha is often used when referring to the tea as a product ready to be consumed, while ichibancha is more appropriate when talking about the harvests. Shincha, or "new tea" from the first flush of the year which is considered the best.

Japan has two distinct tea classifications, sun-grown and shade-grown. Sencha can be either but is called *Kabusecha* (shaded tea) when shaded for around 2 weeks and when shaded longer, 20 days or more, it is called *Gyokuro,* which is considered the finest of the Japanese teas. Sencha may continue to be called sencha even if the leaves are shaded, though in recent years the term "*kabusecha*" (covered tea) commands higher value. Shading increases the chlorophyll production in the plants as the plant tries to capture more light and stops theanine being converted to caffeine. The higher ratio of theanine to caffeine created by shading leads to, not only an improved umami flavoured (savoury) tea, but creates a more relaxed alertness when consumed as the

115

caffeine raises alertness and the theanine calms the mind.

The tea production process differs from Chinese green teas, which are pan-fired, or dry heat roasted by being steamed to kill the green which keeps an emerald green colour in the leaf rather than the olive green of a roasted tea. The flavour profile is markedly different due to the Maillard reaction not having such an effect on steamed tea. The steaming can also be controlled to produce different tea flavours; a short under, 30 seconds steam, is called *asamushi;* the "normal/middle" steam of 30-90seconds is called *chumushi;* a long/deep steam of 1-2 minutes is called *fukamushi*. The long steam lowers astringency, producing a sweeter tea with more body, but also breaks the needle-like leaves so dust can be left in the cup. The Japanese use a special teapot called a kyusu and for fukumushi the pot will have a large mesh strainer, rather than the smaller usual spout leaf strainer.

Following steaming, the leaves are rolled, shaped, and dried creating the characteristic thin, cylindrical shape of the tea. When the tea has been processed it is called aracha and sold to a broker where it is finished by sorting out stems and particles, and the leaves from different farms and fields are blended together. Very little Japanese tea is sold as single estate tea but this is beginning to change as the tea market for high grade tea is becoming more established. Labour costs in Japan are high compared to China so hand made teas can be pricey and much of the good top end Sencha is certainly not cheap, nevertheless, some great machine picked and rolled Sencha can be found for very reasonable prices. Similar to the advice on Long Jing tea, it is recommended initially to buy a reasonable priced Sencha from a reputable supplier and work up the price scale. Japanese teas sometimes appear cloudy in the cup and this is normal and due to the higher than normal amino acid content so is not a steeping defect.

Black Tea

The two teas selected to try are **Darjeeling first flush** and **Assam**. Darjeeling tea is most often made from the AV2 cultivar (Ambi Vari) which is a Chinary hybrid of C. Sinensis var. sinensis, Assam tea is from the large leaved Assam plant Camellia sinensis var. assamica. Both teas are Indian but vastly different terroirs, Darjeeling being high grown in the Himalayan foothills and Assam more sea level grown tea. These two teas show a good range of black tea flavour profiles.

Summarising the *general* difference between a typical Darjeeling tea and a typical Assam tea is as follows:-

- **Variety. Assam is Camellia sinensis var. assamica while Darjeeling is Camellia sinensis var. Sinensis**

- **Altitude. Assam tea is low grown on the plains, Darjeeling is normally, high grown mountain tea.**

- **Oxidation. Assam teas are black teas with full oxidation. Darjeeling teas are called 'black teas' but first flushes are not usually fully oxidised so are closer to oolongs. Some prefer the second flush which has stronger muscatel notes.**

- **Flavour and colour. Assam teas are generally darker in their dry leaf, robust malty flavour and yield a darker cup, Darjeeling teas are known for their floral and fruity muscatel flavour, are more delicate and require a more controlled steep. They are greener in their dry leaf state and give a lighter cup.**

Darjeeling

Darjeeling tea from in West Bengal state is often referred to as "The Champagne of Teas" and much of this tea comes from the AV2 clonal variety. The journey of tea from China to Darjeeling is a fascinating tale of derring-do by Robert Fortune, a tea thief and industrial spy, or a thoroughly decent horticultural man of integrity depending on your point of view, and his exploits are summarised in a book called "For All the Tea in China" by Sarah Rose and is recommended as a good read. Darjeeling is highly prized particularly for the first flush of the season which has a thin bodied, typical light fragrance with a characteristic muscatel flavour, later flushes have more body and stronger flavour where the fragrance of the first flush can be masked. The second flush provides a good example of darjeeling's quality. In examining first flush leaves there is usually a significant amount of green leaf present leading to an opinion that first flush darjeeling tea is nearer an oolong tea than a fully oxidised black tea, something the Darjeeling teamakers might disagree with but the 'rule of tea' seems to be '*10 tea drinkers, 11 opinions!*'. It is important to remember that this is grown in the Himalayan regions so there is slow, low temperature growth early in the season but when the rains come!! - These rains are monsoon deluges leading to rapid plant growth. It has been shown that the abundant sunlight in this high altitude area is responsible for the distinctive flavour of this tea.

- **First flush** harvested in mid-March following spring rains, and has a very light colour, aroma, and mild astringency.

- **Second flush** harvested in June and produces an amber, full bodied, muscatel-flavoured cup.

- **Autumnal flush** is harvested in the autumn after the rainy season, and has somewhat less delicate flavour and less spicy tones, but fuller body and darker colour.

Darjeeling is in North West India high in the Himalayan region where transport is a challenge, the area is prone to earthquakes and soil erosion and there is also political unrest as the local ethnic Gorkhas want independence and often call a general strike called a bandh, which pushes price of tea higher due to low availability. In 2017 the bandh lasted 104 days affecting the 2018 first flush crop.

Assam Tea

For those who like strong coffee, this tea is the strong, robust equivalent in the tea world. Assam tea, manufactured specifically from the plant Camellia sinensis var. Assamica, is lowland grown at, 40-60 metres elevation, near the Brahmaputra River in Assam, India and is known for its body, briskness, malty flavour, and strong, bright colour and the strong flavour. The tea is fully oxidised often by the crush, tear, curl (CTC) process giving massive maceration to the leaf producing the small broken flakes many associate with tea. The climate has a large effect on this tea as the rainfall can be 30 centimetres per day, 3 metres per year from the monsoons, and the heat can achieve 36°C creating a hot, humid, tropical climate that creates a highly flavoured strong tea. Although Camellia sinensis assamica is indiginous to this region it was not until 1834 that this tea plant was recognised as 'tea' even though the indiginous people knew this was so. (To counter any contoversy here – Assam tea plants were *noticed* by Robert Bruce in 1823 but it was only officially recognised and accepted as being tea in 1834 which 'oddly' is the first year of trading that the East India Company did not have a monopoly on the China trade). India is many millenia behind China in modern tea production but has a rapid growth that is challenging China as a dominant tea production area.

This tea is harvested twice in the year, creating two distinct Assam black tea flushes:-

- **Spring Flush** in March until mid-May. The leaf is small and the tea is rich in buds. It is quite rare and unknown. This tea is considered thin, delicate and floral with a light coloured steep. This tea is not really recommended for anything special.
- **Summer Flush** harvest from mid-May onwards is known as tippy tea due to the golden tips on the leaves. This is a sweeter tea, darker, spicy, full-bodied and the superior harvest.

This tea is so highly flavoured that it is associated with milk being added, the typical English style of tea, and also is the basis for Chai spiced tea. It is better to underinfuse this tea or the flavour profile will be wrong being very viscous, too astringent and over bitter. Assam tea is not usually sold as a single estate tea and of those that are single estate none currently come to mind to be singled out, but this tea will be familiar to most black tea drinkers and is usually preferable to a black tea from Kenya.

Oolong (Wulong Tea)

The two teas recommended to try are both Chinese, **Tie Guan Yin** (Iron Goddess of Mercy) generally a lightly oxidised tea so try this first before the heavily baked, roasted tieguanyin tea and **Da Hong Pao** (Big Red Robe) a fuller oxidised tea. They have been chosen as they are both mentioned as tribute teas, teas fit for an emperor, and are vastly different in oxidation and, therefore, flavour profile and colour. There is an enormous amount of different oolongs in flavour and shape and these two have been chosen to represent different ends of the range to illustrate the complexity of this style of tea.,These teas have been chosen but each alone has so many different flavours due to oxidation, roasting and plucking season (spring, summer, autumn) that this tea style alone will keep the curious occupied for some time.

Summarising the *general* difference between a typical **Tie Guan Yin** and a typical **Da Hong Pao** is as follows:-

- The cultivars have a large influence on these teas.

- Tie Guan Yin tends to have more floral notes particularly when lightly oxidised and lightly roasted.

- Tie Guan Yin is typically, but not always, lightly oxidised, on the green side, but Da Hong Pao is usually a more heavily oxidised oolong so is usually a darker oolong.

Tie Guan Yin (Iron Goddess of Mercy)

China has many legends and this tea is no exception. According to legend,there was a rundown temple which held an iron statue of Guanyin, the Bodhisattva of Compassion – she is the lady seen in many Buddhist statues like the Buddha statues. Every day on the walk to his tea fields, a poor farmer named Wei would pass by and reflect on the temple's worsening condition and wanted to help. Being poor, Wei did not have the means to repair the temple so he brought a broom and some incense from his home, swept the temple clean and lit the incense as an offering to Guanyin doing so twice a month. One night, Guanyin appeared to him in a dream, telling him of a cave behind the temple where a treasure awaited which he was to take and share with others. In the cave, the farmer found a tea shoot which he planted in his field and nurtured it into a large bush producing the finest tea. He gave cuttings of this plant to all his neighbours and began selling the tea under the name Tieguanyin. Over time, Wei and all his neighbors prospered, the rundown temple of Guanyin was repaired and became a beacon for the region.

This tea is a lightly oxidised tea, ~20-25% oxidation, originating in Fujian's Anxi County. The cultivar and the tea have the same name, *Tie Guan Yin*, this being the most common variety for Tie Guan Yin but, to confuse matters, Tie Guan Yin can be made from other cultivars, some of which are cross bred with Tie Guan Yin cultivar, but Tie Guan Yin is the 'preferred' cultivar. *Ben Shan* is another very similar cultivar used for Tie Guan Yin although considered to have a less complex flavour so not so good as Tie Guan Yin but is commonly used for oolongs. *Huang Dan* variety, a more floral variety, is made into a Tie Guan Yin style tea and has been cross bred with the Tie Guan Yin variety to produce a popular hybrid called *Huang Guan Yin*.

The plucking is done by taking three or four mature leaves and stems, no buds, so the leaves are quite large. These leaves are sun-wilted for a few hours, a very important step in the process, then taken indoors to complete the withering. Wilted leaves are shaken every few hours and left to oxidised, repeated 3 to 5 times, to bruise the leaf edges to the required level before wok frying or tumble roasting to fix the tea. The time between plucking and fixing is controlled to produce different flavours within this style of tea, a short time (*Zheng Wei*), within the same day or left to the next morning giving characteristic floral notes, or for a longer time of a few days (*Tuo Suan*) which gives more sour notes. The tea is then rolled on a machine to release the juices to quickly release the flavour when the tea is steeped. The leaves are then put into cloth balls tightly rolled, then the ball is opened, the tea ball loosened and the balling process repeated several times each time a little oven drying carried out to dry off the sweated tea. The modern method of making of Tie Guan Yin sometimes involves a step of beating the tea before the next ball rolling to get rid of the red edges, resulting in a less bitter tea with clearer liquid.

There are two subcategories of Tie Guan Yin; *Chuan Tong,* the traditional method, and *Qing Xiang,* the modern method, based on the oxidation level -NOT roasting. The distinction between Chuan Tong, traditional, and Qing Xiang, is whether the tea is traditionally oxidised at natural temperature with more shaking, resulting in heavier oxidation, or at a controlled temperature with less shaking, so lighter oxidation.

Further to this many associate roasting with traditional Tie Guan Yin but the roasting is secondary and sometimes the heavier roast can cover up a multitude of sins but it is the traditional type of Tie Guan Yin. Modern Qing Xiang can be heavily roasted and is called *Nong Xiang Xing Tie Guan Yin,* or heavy Tie Guan Yin, not to be mistaken with the actual traditional Tie Guan Yin. Summarising this:-

> * **Traditional** *(Chuan Tong)* Tie Guan Yin, natural temperature withering/oxidation, heavy shaking, roasted
> * **Modern** *(Qing Xiang)* Tie Guan Yin, controlled temperature withering/oxidation, light shaking, may be roasted

The *Anxi Iron Goddess Tea* is a ball oolong close to a green tea with only a little oxidation and light roasting having a very flowery, fresh delicate aroma character and golden yellow liquor. The *Muzha Iron Goddess Tea* is a traditional oolong, strong roasted and, therefore a stronger taste with a roast nutty character with a reddish-brown liquor.

This brings us to the age old question in tea – is Tie Guan Yin a geographical name, a specific cultivar or a stye of oolong tea. The answer is - all of them so buy a genuine sample from a favoured merchant.

Da Hong Pao (Big Red Robe)

Legend speaks of a scholar who was on his way to the capital to take an imperial examination when he became seriously ill and was forced to stay in the Tian Xin Temple where Buddhist monks helped to restore his health by giving him some of the local tea. The scholar went on to pass his exam, and for this he received a large red robe. To thank the monks for their kindness he presented them with the large red robe with which to cover the tea bushes and thus the tea received its name.

Another legend tells the story of the mother of a Ming Dynasty emperor who became sick and was healed by drinking this tea. To show his gratitude, the emperor sent large red robes to cover the bushes from which the tea was taken. Six of the original bushes, growing on a rock in Jiu Long Ke in Wuyi Shan city on the Wuyi Mountains and reportedly dating back to the Song dynasty, still survive today and are highly venerated. In 2006, the Wuyishan Government stipulated that picking would henceforth be forbidden on the six mother trees. In 2002, a wealthy purchaser paid 180,000 yuan ($28,000) for just 20g of China's Da Hong Pao tea, this really is tea bought with provenance.

Da Hong Pao is an oolong tea from the Wuyi shan (Wuyi Mountain) tea region in Fujian China. Due to the unique soil and natural conditions all teas from the area have a mineral like flavour which is why they are also known as Wuyi Rock teas (*yancha*). These mountains, noted for their ninety nine steep, rugged cliffs and thirty six peaks, are 400 metres above sea level and covered in tea plants giving the 'Famous Four Rock Teas' their name. The terroir is critical to this tea with the cliffs protecting the plants from wind and rain, shade the bushes from too much sunshine and funnel the mists in which the tea plants are bathed. The pure water streams capture the mountain minerals, the winds are channelled between the peaks creating warm days and cool nights making it the perfect tea growing area where different teas grow on each peak.

The cultivar or variety of this tea remains open to debate. The original tribute tea from the original five or six mother tea bushes became very sought after and expensive so plants from them were bred, commonly known as *Qi Dan variety*. Cuttings were taken from these bushes but could not keep up with the demand of an Imperial tea which commands a very high price. Real, true Da Hong Pao comes from the Qi dan variety but in Wuyi Shan, Rou Gui and Shui Xian varieties are now used and blended to make Da Hong Pao. However, it gets more complicated - In the early 1950s Yao Yue Ming started a Da Hong Pao research laboratory using a few stems from the original 800 years old Da Hong Pao tea bushes but his work was interrupted by the cultural revolution so he planted his bushes in the Bei Dou region. This means that the Bei Dou variety may be directly descended hybrids of the original sexually propogated Qi Dan bushes but may also contain other hybrids cross bred into the Qi Dan variety. Qi Dan being originally sexually propogated cannot be a true, genetically pure, cultivar and consequently, neither is Bei Dou. Bei Dou is cloned from different genetic trees 800 year old trees, and furthermore, each tree is likely to have many natural mutations (sports). Taking multiple cuttings from these trees will not be genetically pure and mixing the tree cuttings makes Bei Dou an area name, not clone name for the tea. Does this really matter though as we know that it is the variety and terroir that make this tea and Bei Dou is probably as close as we can now get to the original Qi Dan and we also know that it is the skill of the tea master that processes the tea that makes this good tea special. Bei Dou ("North Star"), Que She (Sparrow's Tongue), and Qi Dan are commonly recognized as close relatives of the original Da Hong Pao trees, aside from Shui Xian and Rou Gui which are sold as Da Hong Pao. There! That's clear then!

Whatever definition is given to Da Hong Pao you will never be able to try the original tea as the trees have been protected since 2006 and are now no longer harvested and there is so much hype on this tea that more Da Hong Pao is sold than the area produces – no surprise there! Even experienced tea drinkers cannot agree on what is authentic but can agree on what is good tea even if not authentic Da Hong Pao.

Puerh

This is one of the most exciting tea categories for tasting sessions. Pu-erh tea in Yunnan province was originally carried and traded for horses or other commodities and the road used for this trade was called "The Ancient Tea Horse Road". During the long journey, exposure to moisture from rain, resulted in a natural post-fermentation and the resulting ageing and post-fermentation process, created a tea which was said to aid digestion, provide important nutrients and had a unique taste.

These teas are best using one gram of tea per 15ml water or about 7-8 grams per 100 ml teapot and using boiled water. This seems a lot of tea but a good tea session with a good puerh will give 10-15 steeps with the rise and fall in flavour intensity and character as well and the change from floral through full bodied to sweet can be enjoyed. Yunnan sourcing is the best place to buy puerh tea but others such as Moylor are very reliable suppliers – for details see recommended suppliers, Chapter 12. This 'genre' of tea can be quite a delight for investigating. The prices can also be very confusing so, to begin with, it is advisable not to pay too much. Fine puerh tea can be purchased from a few pounds to several hundred pounds so try the lower price end – but not too low! Now the tricky part – this tea is usually better the older it becomes but a poor tea will never be a good aged tea so the start point is vital. Like a vintage wine, those who can identify a good puerh for storage will be able to pick up a bargain if purchased as a new tea. Collectors will buy tea and lay down a good tea stash for the future – or their grandchildren! This is a mould produced tea and sometimes the mould can be seen. This is not a defect but part of the tea.

Xishuang Banna is famous for pu-erh tea due to the fact that it was the origin of the ancient tea route, however, many other places in Yunnan also produce pu-erh tea. Most of the pu-erh tea production areas were developed either along the mountain, like Wu Liang Shan, Ai Lao Shan and Da Xue Shan, or it was developed along the river, like Mekong River. There are four major regions producing pu-erh - Xishuang Banna, Lin Cang, Pu-erh, Chang Ning and the four most famous factories are - Kun-ming, Meng-hai, Xia-guan and Lin-chang. Look for these names and try a selection as it is possible to buy small samples of these teas rather than the whole bing so not too much a drain on the pocket to sample 5 or 6 different puerhs. There are two sub-varieties of this tea with different characteristics to try:-

Raw (_shengcha_), the original and arguably the best puerh, is naturally aged and matured for several years. High prices can be paid for a good aged sheng but age alone does not command the price it must be a good, high quality tea as the taste is crucial to justify the high price. Three years ageing is considered minimum for this tea to bring out the flavour correctly but some shengs like wine, continue to improve up to twenty years and beyond. Sheng can be made from green or white tea compressed into the final shape

There is much discussion as to when a shengcha made from green tea becomes a 'black tea'. As the green tea ages it turns darker brown, similar to light coloured oak wood becoming black in ancient buildings, but Puerh tea is marketed as 'black tea' even when it is young and still green. To prepare this tea a chunk of tea is peeled off from the compressed block with special puerh knives which can be bought for this purpose although any penknife will suffice. It is a strong, complex flavoured tea that will last for many steeps with differing flavour profiles as subsequent infusions change the flavour profile and the water temperature can never be too hot for this robust tea. This is the joy of puerh tea and makes it the most interesting tea to drink. A quick internet search shows the variety of sheng puerh available such as white, purple, ancient tree (gushu).

Ripe or cooked (*shoucha/shucha*) Shou cha is most definitely dark tea and makes a liquor that is very dark. Shous undergoes accelerated fermentation where the leaves are piled and ~30% water is added in a warm room to *ferment* the tea for several months, in which time the pile becomes heated like a compost effect, hence the term *cooked.* then the tea can then be sold as loose puerh tea or pressed into into various shapes to produce "ripe/cooked" shoucha. The leaves usually come from young plantation bushes which, by their nature, are grown more intensively close together with modern farming techniques using fertilisers and insecticides so will never have the uniqueness of wild or ancient trees. This ripening process is called Wu Dui ripening and was developed in 1973 by the Kunming and Meng Hai Tea Factories to imitate and speed up the process of ageing Sheng. Ageing will not really add much to this tea as it is ready to drink immediately.

Typical compressed puerh tea

128

CHAPTER TEN

TEA PRICING (KNOW YOUR SUPPLIER!)

Many people who decide to buy a good quality tea are surprised and initially put off by the price of some high end teas. The issue is not why it is so expensive but how is it so cheap for everyday tea? Pricing good teas is a minefield leading to the question of how is good, genuine tea sourced, what price should be paid, and is the price of the tea 'cheap' or 'inexpensive'? Teas are priced by a number of factors such as exceptional taste, manufacturing and transport costs, demand for the particular tea, rarity and provenance but paying exceptional money for an average tea is something to be avoided. The price of tea and the quality of the cup experience are not always directly related, which means some very expensive teas can be good but not exceptional, and some inexpensive teas can be excellent. A quick internet search will show, for example, two puerhs side by side one for $300 and the other for $25 making a comparison of the two an expensive proposition and, with little opportunity to taste the teas, to know whether the the higher price tea is that much better. Generally, if a tea is too cheap for the type of tea advertised it is probably not authentic and getting it wrong hurts the pocket. Do not confuse inexpensive with cheap as some teas may seem expensive but may actually represent very good value to a connoisseur. Actually, being pragmatic, if you like the taste of the tea – fine! Does it matter? The answer being that only when you feel you have overpaid for a special tea that fails to deliver is this an issue. Always note that *authentic* and *original* are not the same thing and always remember that really good quality tea is never cheap but it may be inexpensive!

> **Money cannot buy happiness but it can buy tea which is the same thing!**

There is a base price where the plantation owner needs to make a living by charging commercially acceptable prices before adding on any premium for special high quality, skill demand, provenance or scarcity. A search on tea prices in the UK market found a supermarket tea for a retail price of ~£3/Kg, and this tea was in a teabag with all the additional costs of packing into a teabag, up to a top quality Long Jing Ming Qian offered by a 'wholesaler' with a price of £530/Kg with transport, taxes and retail profit margin still to be added! I have blind tasted teabag tea from the cheapest to the mid-range supermarket teas and, without doubt, the cheap tea is exactly that – cheap, acrid, astringent, thin – mid range teas can be okay for an everyday drink - the top end of the mass market is preferable everyday beverage that would not cause embarrassment by serving to guests. Occassionally, pay more money and try a real high end tea from a reputable supplier and discover what tea can really offer.

Long Jing green tea is graded, premium and from Grade 1-6, premium being the best. Much of the grading is on the leaf appearance - no stalks, even size whole leaf, even good colour and other physical attributes. Buying a lower grade tea is much cheaper but not necessarily an inferior tasting cup quality. If one particular tea is sorted and 10% stalks removed but the cost of labour pushes the price up 20% then you may not wish to pay the premium for a good looking tea but you may have to put in a little more tea to make the same taste. It is often preferable to buy a lower grade of a very good tea than a high grade lesser tea. Do not be put off by the price of a good quality tea. Puerh cakes can be purchased for £25 to £300 for a 375g bing so using 7-8gms of puerh tea in a 175ml teapot and infusing the tea ten to fifteen times makes a good tea session of ~50 steeps which is 500-750 cups per cake. The choice becomes whether the £25 tea is not quite so good as the more expensive but is it okay for an everyday tea treat, the focus being on cup taste versus cost. Good quality expensive leaf tea is reserved for that special moment in the day and the *very* expensive tea for that very special occasion!!!

Production costs

Consider mass market tea and compare these with high grade speciality tea and note the economies of scale, the labour cost of the process, transport costs. High labour costs (Really!) have led to unscrupulous, exploitative practices taking place on some plantations which persist to this day and only investigative journalism and internet communications is now exposing this practice for big industry to be sufficiently, commercially embarrassed to take positive steps to remedy. Some big international companies regrettably still have issues and note that in 2018 workers received daily wage of between 145 and 167 rupees ($1.94) per day, just above half the state-mandated daily wage of 250 rupees ($3.54) for unskilled labourers, and around one third of the minimum wages advisory board for tea workers in Assam had stipulated which is 360 rupees. The state government failed to implement the Minimum Wages Act in tea plantations and wages are set to rise in 2019 by 30 rupees! Before deciding to only buy FairTrade tea, Oxfam and the Ethical Tea Partnership found their workers wages were no higher than non Fair Trade tea plantations! Below is a picture of an Indian tea picker - see how happy she is!!!

Image by pen_ash from Pixabay

Traditionally, the leaves are hand picked by workers carrying huge baskets on their backs, a very labour-intensive process whereas mass market tea is grown on flat ground with plantations of neat rows so mechanical harvesting is possible. Large, two man hedge cutters are pulled along the bushes' top leaves where the cutters slice the flush, netting up to ten times more tea compared to a hand-picker who averages ~20Kg a day - 20Kg of picked leaves leads to ~5Kg of finished tea or less. Leaf damage occurs but is acceptable for black teas because after withering the leaves will be fully macerated to achieve maximum oxidation, dried as quickly as possible and mechanically sorted to remove the unwanted parts. It is interesting to note that "big tea" is supportive of international workers rights now that they are "big tea" and so have invested in machinery to reduce labour costs and hopefully look after their reduced workforce better. However, labour reduction inevitably leads to fears that tea workers jobs will become obsolete with no alternative employment opportunities for the workers. Some teas that rely on labour, such as ball rolled oolongs, can be higher priced in a high cost labour region for example comparing Taiwan oolongs with Chinese mainland oolongs.

High grade teas are grown on mountain sides where transport and harvesting are difficult but these are the very conditions that favour good tea. Hand plucking is also necessary to achieve the desired plucking standard and this inevitably means lower yields than mechanical shaving, so much higher labour, plucking and transport costs. Some white tea can only be picked for a few hours at, or before, dawn if weather conditions permit so the yield is limited to a few kilos per day, the lower yield again pushing up the price.

Following a controlled wither, sometimes outside in the sun if weather permits, or indoors noting the airflow through the room and the daily humidity, the leaves are mechanically rolled or for the very best teas hand rolled. Small artisanal estates hand roll with experienced, skilled tea makers who can manipulate the leaves in a very controlled way where no amount of chemical testing has ever replaced the nose and taste buds of these skilled artisans so again labour and skill, the expensive art, makes the price higher but generally a better tea. Jasmine teas are made using jasmine buds which are picked just as they are ready to open and are layered in the tea. During this time, the buds pop open and release the fragrance to the tea when they are removed and replaced with fresh jasmine buds, a process repeated four or five times, then the leaves are rolled to make pearls to retain the fragrance. The labour costs of this process is enormous compared with lobbing in a few flowers and selling the mixture as jasmine tea. No mass product can compare to a highly skilled tea master making hand processed tea.

Big business can control the land whereas a Chinese farmer has smaller estates and complex communist landownership laws where the farmer never fully owns the land and multi-generational ownership of land is unheard of. Part of the tea problem is that the farmer cannot pass the land onto the next generation as they have to purchase the land. In some famous tea regions big business can price the artisanal family farmer out of the market and then demand higher prices to cover the investment. This is the case with land around Hangzhou and West Lake, home ofLong Jing tea, where big business has bought whole hillsides areas displacing multi generational families who are left with litttle land near Huangzhou, China's fourth largest city, so a far cry from artisanal tea making. Some of the finest teas come from mountain, clean air and water areas, which are the very areas to which the Chinese government has given protected status meaning expansion of the estates is impossible. The, is very desirable area sought after by big-business which boasted 153 billionnaires in 2017. "Up in heaven, there is paradise down on earth, there is Hangzhou". With its canals and waterways, hills, temples, Longjing tea plantations, Xixi

National Wetland Park and the world-renowned West Lake, Hangzhou has built a reputation as one of the most beautiful cities in China. The pressure on land for tea is enormous and with the reputation of tea from this region the price of tea is very high.

Authenticity

A general rule is that if the tea is too cheap it almost certainly means it is neither authentic nor high-quality. Non-authentic tea is a huge plague to the industry but efforts are becoming to be put in place to protect origin-specific goods which are known as geographical indications or appellations. Geographical indications are defined by the World Trade Organization's TRIPS agreement to be - *"indications which identify a good as originating in the territory of a World Trade Organization member, or a region or locality in that territory, where a given quality, reputation or other characteristic of the good is essentially attributable to its geographical origin"* TRIPS Article 22. An example of this is Cheddar cheese originally made in Cheddar but became a style of cheese made anywhere, however, in this example, European laws now dictate that such geographical names can only be used by the authentic product made in Cheddar. This still does not mean that the cheese made in Cheddar is the best as there are some very good similar cheeses on the market from other countries but they cannot be called 'cheddar'. There are efforts in tea producing countries to overcome this issue with designated labelling but this is in its infancy and not well regulated, largely because tea is traded in bulk, which makes traceability difficult to prove.It is not just Chinese tribute teas that suffer authenticity claims as there is more Darjeeling sold in the market than is produced in Darjeeling. In 2004, the amount of tea sold as Darjeeling worldwide exceeded 40,000 tonnes but the annual tea production of Darjeeling is estimated at only 10,000 tonnes some of the difference coming from Nepal trading on the

Darjeeling name.

Logos indicating authentic origin

Darjeeling now has geographical protection and the logo is applied on genuine Darjeeling teas so is something to look for (unless, of course, the logo is also fake!). Nepal now has its own logo and geographical protection status. The only advice to overcome this problem is to purchase tea from a known, reputable supplier and enjoy the tea experience!

Non-authentic tea may just be non-original tea. Lapsang Souchong tea mentioned previously, originally made in Tongmu village in Wuyi mountains in Fujian Provine, China, commands a high price which encourages copies which may be, and often are, inferior teas.

Around the time of the Beijing Olympics in 2008 puerh tea was much in demand and prices soared for puer teas. It is easy to change wrappers on puerh teas which undoubtedly occurred where cheap puerh was rewrapped in the same packaging as a top quality puerh and sold at top quality prices. Reputable suppliers are key to avoiding this pitfall of fraud in the tea industry. Another example is Xi Hu Long Jing Shi Feng tea considered to be highly prized West Lake tea making this tea high priced. The premium tea from jiangtea.com is $580/Kg providing a clear temptation for unscrupulous vendors on some websites to make a lot of money by switching the consignment to a lower grade Long Jing tea. So if cheap offers are found they may be fakes, but most Long Jing teas are wonderful and many are very reasonably priced for everyday tea and just a little dearer for special occassion tea, soresearch before buying.

Demand

There is a tradition in Asia of giving tea as a gift and in China tea is one of the finest and most appropriate gifts to be offered as a sign of respect so the finer the tea, the finer the gift. More often than not, when tea is bought directly from China there is a little gift included in the parcel, usually tea. Teas meant for the Emperor of Imperial China and his court are accorded the status of *Tribute Teas* or *Gong Cha* similar to the term 'By Royal Appointment" in the UK. These tribute teas would be the best teas except that as demand for them increases so does the price which can be quite high.

One famous tribute tea, Da Hong Pao which originally came from five ancient trees but is now no longer available to buy at any price. The five original trees were cloned and clones were taken of the daughter clones. The mother trees always command higher prices than the cloned trees, in this case due to provenance, but the frst generation clones command higher prices than second and so on to the third generation and beyond but they are all being marketed as if they were the original five tribute trees, Da Hong Pao becoming a marketing name. One purchaser in 2002 paid $28,000 for 20 grams of original Qi Dan Da Hong Pao making it one of the most expensive teas in the world - see below for a fuller description of Da Hong Pao.

A further, but less extreme example, of the tea buying minefield is the higher price Ming Qian, early spring tea, commands when only the supplier will know whether it is genuine spring tea until it is tasted or a tea expert confirms the tea. Personally, I am delighted with a low price Long Jing but having compared it with a spring plucked Long Jing twice the price I am happy to buy both, one for everyday tea and the other for occasional use and guests. If you ask whether the higher priced tea is really Ming Qian I have no idea except that it makes a better cup than the lower priced tea and I rely on my Chinese supplier, so suppliers do need choosing with care. I have had failures where I have bought a medium price Jin Jun Mei, knowingly too cheap to be authentic, which was okay but not up to authentic taste standards when compared with an expensive tea from a very reputable supplier. That is the nature of tea drinking and the adventure that tea drinking will give. Even when you have found a good tea curiosity will lead to buying a similar tea for more money which may be even better (or not)! Of course, tea is a natural product and one year I found a delightful tea which doubled in price the following year because other buyers had also found it and the price rose accordingly, the year after that it was not available at all due to rain during the short plucking season this tea had.

Demand for scarce, rare teas will also influence price for a particular tea. Yellow tea is quite scarce so the price of a authentic, good quality, yellow tea can be quite high and unrelated to whether you believe it is an exceptional tea or not, similarly, an exceptional white tea should be plucked before the sun has risen too far and chlorophyll affects the bud, and also on a dry day meaning that some years there is little or no crop. The grower charges a higher price just because of scarcity. Anji Bai Cha has a very good reputation, is more expensive than many other similar teas due to the exceptional taste it delivers, and is often bought as a status tea by many wealthy Chinese pushing up the price. It has a 'snob value' where the price/quality ratio is often skewed to a higher price due to demand rather than just quality.

Authentic Lapsang Souchong originates in Tongmu, which is now a protected area in Wuyishan mountain area, so it is not possible to expand the tea growing area or the area from which to source the specific wood that the smoke is made from. Tongmu, as a result, is now becoming famous for another tea called Jin Jun Mei but this also now suffers the same problems in that it is a very good tea, has limited supply and is copied in areas far from Tongmu with these other areas still charging the premium price of a genuine Tongmu Lapsang Souchong. So buyer beware and <u>buy all tea from a reputable supplier</u>.

Marketing

Marketing of teas is a minefield in itself. There are so many ridiculous claims for some teas that it is quite discreditable. For example, Da Hong Pao is marketed as being one of the most expensive teas, but many other teas also lay claim to this irrelevent boast which appears to suggest that the high price the vendor expects is actually cheap when compared to what could be charged by the best tea, in the best year, to someone who has too much money. The high price also says nothing about the taste or quality of the tea.

There are many spurious health claims and it would appear from many vendors that drinking tea will cure all the ills of mankind, reduce weight, protect your heart and circulation, reduce cancers and be the elixir of life, indeed a miracle substance. Some claims may be true but many are not scientifically proven and any proven effect is usually so small it is not significant or it occurs *in vitrio (test tube)* but not in vivo (in the body). One example of these claims is matcha tea being a rich source of EGCG,a powerful, very reactive antioxidant and as the leaf and liquor are both consumed the antioxidant intake is very high. Many of these claims are based on 'in-vitrio' studies (in a test tube) and on this basis seem very plausable, however, 'in-vivo' (in the body/cell) many of the studies fall down. Matcha is frothed up like a latte type coffee so EGCG will start reacting and losing effect before ingestion, then it will oxidise in the stomach before passing to the intestines where it is absorbed into the bloodstream, all the time losing potency. It is such a large molecule that it is unclear how much is actually absorbed into the bloodstream and after absorption it has to get to the target organ to have any benefit. Studies are encouraging but not yet highly convincing, however,Matcha tea is widely reported as reducing breast cancer cells, perhaps in glass, but do not rely on these claims for your body. Remember – Tea may not make you healthy but it certainly will not make you unhealthy.

> **Do not drink tea for health reasons drink it because you like it.**

Reputation

China has many tea competitions where the farmer submits a few kilograms of tea to be judged with the opportunity of being awarded a gold medal status and consequently command a high price. Much care goes into the submitted sample but other tea of the same name from the same supplier will not necessarily be the same standard as the competition grade. It will, however enhance the reputation of the producer who clearly knows the tea process well enough to have the skill to produce a fine tea. Other growers in the village may try to cash in on the act and market their product as originating from a particular village or region that produces gold medal winning tea, or by claiming this named tea recently sold for a very high price but we offer special batches for pocket money. The name then becomes corrupted to a 'style' of tea which may not be the authentic tribute or gold medal tea. These other teas may be inferior, equally good rarely better but they are not the authentic tea and this should be reflected in the price. Taking, as an example, the famous Chateauneuf-du-Pape vintage wine on the internet, one bottle cost £995 another £60. Most wine drinkers do not have the money to compare the two but even if they did it I would have to be a special connoisseur to justify paying the higher price. So it is with tea - stay in your comfort zone!

Chinese Tea Grading System

Just like the Indian system of grading teas by leaf physical attributes, the Chinese also have such a system where the highest grade will have less damage, dust, stalks etc. but the grade says little about the cup quality. Chinese teas are usually numbered from '1' the highest grade downward. Generally 7 or 8 is what most people deal with bur again, this grading is specific to the leaf style and shape.

In addition to numbering, reference is made to the season of harvest in the Chinese system. Pre-qingming Dragonwell ("before the rains") is a good example of this. Certain seasons yield better quality of flavour, in general, so where this is significant, it is mentioned.

Excellent tea is relatively expensive, because processing is done by hand. Although handmade tea production is relatively small, its flavour is 'artisanal' and variable but usually higher quality than machine made tea. Machine manufactured tea is produced in large quantity so the process is cheaper but may not produce the full fragrance potential during the process.

When it comes to grade and quality the following prices illustrate why tea prices differ so much if only the headline type of tea is mentioned. In the following wholesale Da Hong Pao example Zhengyan is in the core production area of the finest Wuyi rock tea area whereas Banyan is an original but not core area. The point to notice is the price difference between the regions and between the grades of tea, an almost tenfold difference, showing that the grade of the tea has a major impact on price. A good supplier will always tell customers exactly what they are selling.

• Premium 1	Zhengan	$470 / £376
• Premium 2	Zhengan	$360 / £288
• Grade 1	BanYan	$203 / £162
• Grade 2	BanYan	$150 / £120
• Grade 3	BanYan	$85 / £68
• Grade 4	BanYan	$53 / £42

Organic

Organic teas are becoming increasingly popular and the popularity is reflected in the price. Many consumers are rightly nervous about unknown suppliers in China using too much insecticide which may fall foul of European laws or personal preferences for completely insecticide free tea. Puerh tea is a notable example where the source of the leaves sometimes indicates whether the tea is herbicide and insecticide free.

- **Plantation bushes are densely planted so insecticides are used so unlikely to be organic products.**
- **"Wild arbour" trees or old plantations that have reverted to feral trees may be pesticide free**
- **Wild trees (gŭshù, literally old tree) - pesticide free**

Provenance

Tea has history and this reflects in the price of many teas. If the tea is a tribute tea it has the 'seal of approval' like a royal warrant in the UK. If an emperor likes a particular tea the price rises as does the esteem of the tea maker. These days, although six Qi Dan trees are the original Da Hong Pao leaves it is impossible to buy this tea as the teas are now protected and picking has been banned. Prior to this, pre 2006, tourists could catch a few leaves and make this special tea but this is now impossible. One needs little imagination to realise that the tea commandef a very high price and the local vendors were known to sell more Da Hong Pao Qi Dan than is physically possible.

Summary

So how do you purchase a good tea? The advice is to not place too much emphasis on authenticity until you have a reputable supplier but focus on the quality of the tea in the cup. Buy medium price teas from reputable suppliers initially, possibly the most expensive you can reasonably afford, identify what you like and compare it with other similar teas to make your value judgment of whether the price difference is worth paying. The best suppliers will to provide information about the tea such as season, origin, cultivar, elevation, production method, estate, date of picking and name of plantation, and include pictures of the dry and wet leaf. Buying in person is the best way and reputable suppliers will let you taste their teas. I once spent two hours in a shop in Hong Kong tasting tea but most of the time we have to rely on online shopping which is both a boon and a minefield. If you do take time with a vendor this it is only polite to buy some tea as there will always be a notable tea with a good vendor.

Modern farming and tea making practises mean that the distinctions that may have originally existed between true geographic, or tribute teas are less important than in the past so it is better not to be caught up in the marketing hype but to source on personal taste experience and guidance from experienced trusted tasters. Take care with marketing claims, buy from a reputable supplier and judge by cup quality. Please note that tea is best consumed for organoleptic enjoyment as most health claims are generally unproven, overstated or wrong.

CHAPTER ELEVEN

TEA PREPARATION

In the preceding chapters it should be noted that tea is not *fermented*, this being a term incorrectly and widely used, it is *oxidised* and similarly, tea is not *brewed* it is *infused or steeped*. Fermenting and brewing are fine terms in beer and wine making but we are dealing with tea so oxidising and steeping, or infusing, should be used.

What can be so difficult in putting hot water on a few tea leaves for a short time and drinking the liquor? The answer is nothing! It is a simple process and the only challenge is to bring the best out in the tea for one's own personal preference. There is a great deal of conflicting recommendations in books and the internet on how to prepare a cup of tea and some are quite confusing, such as those that recommend one or two teaspoons of tea in a cup of water. The variation in tea shapes mean a teaspoon can be anything from 1-4 grams of tea, and exactly what volume is "a cup" is confusing to someone trying an expensive tea for the first time. General principles are given here and what affects the tea we taste, but the best recommendation is to make the tea the way you like it and if you are trying a new tea then make it in a standard way that you have come to prefer. Below is a recommended standard method to begin to learn a new tea and this can be varied as the tea is understood.

The variables in tea preparation available are basically:-

- **Choice of leaf tea,**
- **Ratio of leaf to water,**
- **Temperature of the water**
- **Time of steeping :-**

Leaf & Water Choice

See recommendations in Chapter 9 as a starting point for the leaf. Tea is mainly water and many studies show that tea liquors extracted using purified water gave better flavour than tap water particularly if chlorinated. so mineral water for expensive teas may be best. The tea is the star of the show. That notwithstanding, water is important but normal tap water is good for most teas unless you have a particularly strange tasting local water or do blind tea tasting sessions of hard water, soft water and bottled water to test your preferences. Hard water contains minerals that changes tea flavour so this becomes something for personal discovery. Some say do not over-boil, or reboil, the water as it becomes de-oxygenated and, whilst de-oxygenation does occer, it takes an experienced tea taster to identify this effect which can easily be overcome by pouring water from a height in a splashy manner thereby re-oxygenating the water. Most literature for Chinese tea states that you should not boil the water like a raging torrent or reboil the water so, to achieve the correct temperature of hot water, raise the heat to the required temperature this advice being handed down from Lu Yu in the first tea book written in 780A.D. Japanese tea experts from the Japanese Tea Export Council believe that bubbles form in water on a heat source leading to a variable infusion due to the water not being fully in contact with the leaf, so their advice is to boil the water and leave it to cool to the desired temperature. There is not really a discernible difference but some may disagree - it appears to be more of a difference of opinion between the Chinese and the Japanese styles.

Leaf quantity

The ratio of leaf to tea is so crucial to tea enjoyment that it is important to know the approximate size of the brewing vessel so as a guide to approximate capacities of drinking vessels, a Chinese teacup is 50mls or less, English teacup is ~125mls, a mug is 225mls. The way to measure the leaf quantity is to know what quantity of tea to the pot gives a satisfactory cup but in the case of whole leaf, which cannot be measured by a teaspoon, this is difficult so getting a feel for a 'pinch' of tea is the best way. Due to the different number of teas that may be taken it is an advantage to purchase a small electronic scale which can be found on ebay for a few pounds/dollars and then a sample pinch will act as a future guide. It is the quantity of tea per 100 mls which is most important but NEVER have too little tea in the water as it is better to err on using too much rather than too little but this can make controlling the time of brew more critical as a few seconds too long on the steep with a high ratio of leaves can spoil the taste profile. All things being equal, if two infusions are made with, for example, 1g of leaf/100ml water and compared with 4g/100ml the thickness, brothiness, viscosity will increase making a richer, creamier tea: Bitterness and astringency will increase which is desirable up to a point when it can become unpleasantly acrid and overpower the high floral notes: The high floral notes will be more pronounced in a short steep time but will be overpowered very quickly by the bitterness so controlling the balance of flavour between aroma relies on good steep time control.

A rough guide to start is :-

- **Green tea 3 - 3.5 gms**
- **Oolongs 4 - 4.4 gms**
- **Red/Black tea 3 gms**
- **Puerh 5-6 gms**

Summarising below as leaf quantity increases from left to right:-

- Texture –Thin   -   More Texture
- Flowery aromatic   -   Bitterness, Astringency

145

- Weak overall flavour   -   Strong flavour
- Delicate aroma noticeable   -   Strong overpowering taste
- Economic   -   More expensive
- More control of infusion   -   Less infusion control
- Delicate flavour   -   Robust flavour

Time of Infusion

One thing that cannnot happen is that **brewing half the quantity for twice as long does not make the same tea.** The flavour profile changes from a light, delicate floral cup to a more robust, complex flavour profile as the deeper notes infuse into the steep and begin to overpower the delicate citrousy, floral notes.

Summarising with increasing times from left to right:-

- Flavour complexity narrow   -   More complex flavour
- Weak flavour   -   Stronger flavour
- Bitterness, Astringency low   -   More bitterness
- Aromatics   -   Robust flavours

Water Temperature

The water temperature is important due to the hundreds of chemicals that produce the flavour of tea being extracted at different rates, so a hot infusion will extract more bitter catechins and methylxanthines which override the light, delicate fragrances, however, a cool infusion will preserve the fragrances but the briskness and bitter notes will not be fully developed. A general principle is the more delicate the tea the cooler the water and this favours multiple infusions but to be a little more specific :-

- **Japanese Gyokuro 50°C**
- **White teas are best at 60-70°C**
- **Green at 80-85°C**
- **Black robust teas 95+°C**
- **Puerh teas 95+°C**

Always remember, the cooler the water the longer the tea can be steeped to bring out a good balanced flavour and in the case of Japanese gyokuro, a high quality green shaded tea, 50°C is recommended in order to bring out the umami flavour without too much overpowering bitterness.

Many tea drinkers infuse tea using the cold infusion method which is to put the leaves in room temperature water and then put the infusion vessel in the fridge overnight and drinking the tea as acold drink thus keeping the delicate floral notes – Try it!

Temperature control is mainly about controlling the bitterness and astringency such that it does not overpower the delicate aromas and umami flavour.

Summarising with increasing temperatures from left to right:-

- Flora, fruity, delicate aromas- More bitterness/astringent

Put it all together

The relationship between leaf quantity, time and temperarure is due to the interaction of the chemicals in the tea that contribute to the flavour. When water hits the leaf the soluble chemicals begin to dissolve into the water. Aroma chemicals are light and quickly dissolve in the water but larger or less soluble chemicals take a little longer, such as caffeine and some large polyphenols which contribute to bitterness. All things being equal, tea making is bitterness control:

- If the **time of steep** is short duration then the tea will tend to be more floral, aromatic. Longer steeps allow bitter notes to enter the liquor and overpower the lighter notes. Too long on the steep means a very bitter or astringent tea. Balance of flavours is the desired outcome.

- If the **temperature of the water** is too high then the time to stop the extraction wil be very short and not easily controllable and the bitters will quickly overpower the overall taste of the florals. Some tea drinkers refer to this as scalding the tea.

- If the **quantity of tea** is too little tea then the high floral notes will not be sufficient in quantity to be above the flavour threshold for detection by our senses but iff too much then bitter notes will overpower the delicate fragrances

So, plenty of tea - short steeps – water not too hot

This gives two distinct styles of tea making, the western way, of putting in a small quantity of leaf for a few minutes, the other, the oriental way is putting in a large amount of leaf and infusing for a few seconds, This latter method allows for several infusions, the number of infusions possible being roughly correlated to the quality of the tea. The following is recommended as a start point for tea tasting but note that broken orange pekoe is small tea particles and many of the teas will be whole leaf so the infusion will take a little longer on a whole leaf compared to that of a broken orange pekoe of small particle size. Additionally, a 'pearl' tea shape such as jasmine pearls, or gunpowder tea, will be tightly curled to lock in the flavour so these may take even longer to infuse than open whole

148

leaf so these teas need 'waking up' by an initial wash of a few seconds. The reason for the tight curl is to prevent the higher note volatiles escaping during storage so a balance needs to be found between time of infusion to develop the cup favour and not losing too much of the higher fragrances. This is one reason for the Chinese method of infusing where small teapots are used with lots of tea and multiple short infusions. Part of the tea journey will be to notice how the flavour changes, rising with each subsequent infusion until the tea is exhausted and the flavour fades away but red tea is not so good for multiple infusions.

- Western Tea Style: 1.5 grams of tea to 100ml water for 2-3 minutes steep

- Chinese Tea Style: 3-5 grams of tea to 100ml water, 30 second initial infusion and on subsequent infusions raise the water temperature and/or infusion time a little on each subsequent infusions. <u>This is, by far, the best method for a tea drinking session.</u>

- Puerh tea is usually best made Chinese style putting ~5 grams of tea in 100-125ml pot, a 10 second rinse to remove dust and wake up the leaves then infuse for ~20-30 seconds to begin with. A reasonable puerh can easily give 6+, a good puerh 15+ infusions making a wonderful tea session.

Recommended Tea Preparation

The following instructions will help you to make a good cup of any kind of tea. This is a starting point where times, temperatures and tea/water ratio can be varied to suit your taste.

- Bring water to a boil in a kettle
- When water is at a gentle boil, remove heat.

- Pour hot water into the teapot and pour this water into the teacups then discard the water. This warms the tea ware so the water temperature will be more consistent.

- Add 3g green/black tea, 4g oolong, 5g heicha tea leaves **(Do not make the mistake of using too little!)** to 100mls water. Do not skimp on the tea it is better to put 3.5 grams in than 2.5 grams. I have found it helpful to weigh the the tea for the first few time using small, inexpensive scales commonly found on ebay for a few pounds/dollars, when trying a new tea as a guide for the future.

- Allow the water to cool to the desired temperature, if necessary, and pour over the tea leaves. Chinese style preparation involves washing the leaves by discarding after the first few seconds infusion and then proceeding with the recommended infusion times. This washes and 'wakes up' the leaf and is always recommended for Puerh tea.

- Infuse for 30 seconds to one minute depending on your taste – I use one minute for a new tea to bring out the flavours and 'learn the tea' but 30 seconds is all that is needed for fragrant oolongs or delicate white tea. However, white tea can be steeped for up to five minutes to develop a personally desired flavour.

- Pour completely into cups to prevent over infusing, or optionally into a jug known as a fairness cup in the Chinese gong fu tea making method.

- For multiple infusion, raise the water temperature and increase the infusion times

Any recommendations for making a cup of tea are exactly that – *recommendations*. Included above are rough start points but for each individual the best way to make tea is like the name of the famous play by Shakespeare, **"As You Like It"**.

Before beginning, some mention should be given to the tea infusing vessel and the cup in which it is served as part of the tea appreciation and enjoyment, for example, do you really want to drink a fine wine from a jam jar or teacup, beer in a tea mug or tea in a paper cup which does not do justice to the experience. When drinking tea always use teapots and cups that are appropriate to the tea.

So now put aside the teabag and the mug, invest in a personal teapot and thin walled teacup, or even one of those small tea cups used by Chinese or Japanese tea drinkers, pay a little more for your tea and learn to make and enjoy fine tea but **do not add anything** – learn to enjoy the taste of tea.

Tea Tasting

Firstly, a few tips on the best way to enjoy tea. Do not be put off by the colour of the infusion which may be much lighter than what you are used to. Green tea infusions tend to be yellow or pale straw coloured(It's the flavonols) and look a little weak so do not be deceived by the unfamiliar colour. The colour is something that a tea drinker gets used to and as the colour is different for each tea it can be used as a quality indicator of what is to come. White tea infusions will be almost colourless or pale straw but full of flavour so do not judge a tea just by colour alone.

Many British tea drinkers try green tea but initially do not like it and this is often because the perception of what tea should taste like is not met. My advice is to exclude milk and sugar then infuse the tea quite by putting the same amount as normal in the brewing vessel but infusing for a very short time which is explained below in a little more detail. The best way to enjoy the taste of tea is without milk or sugar which is not to say that with these additions the tea tasting experience is lesser but to properly detect the full flavour experience that tea can deliver it is preferable without additions. This may be a big step and strange at first but once the pallet is attuned to true tea taste it is difficult to go back to the European standard of having milk and/or sugar. Something to note is that worldwide lactose intolerance is very high with estimates in excess of 70%, in Asian, African and Inuit ethnic groups and around 25% in European and American groups. Most animals lose the enzyme lactase, required to metabolise lactose, when they stop breast feeding. Humans did this naturally around the age of around five years old, so the lactose passes through the digestive system to the gut where gut flora are able to process lactose but in so doing create gas as a bi-product leading to bloating, diarrhoea and wind. It is believed that a genetic mutation occurred in man in Sweden that now allows humans to process lactose which is why the highest lactose tolerant ethnic group tends to be white Europeans. Note that Chinese are largely dairy intolerant which is why dairy items do not feature in their diets.

So why do we add sugar? There are two reasons for this one being that increasing sugar concentrations make caffeine molecules aggregate (clump) together so the tea becomes less bitter as a result. In addition to this, bitter and sweet receptors on the tongue interact with each other[18] so they have a mutual masking effect where increasing sweetness actually turns off the tongue's bitter receptor. This can work the other way round if the bitterness is higher than the sweetness factor. Actually, the most effective way of reducing bitterness in tea or coffee is to add a few grains of salt which is a very effective way to turn off or block the bitter receptors on the tongue. Lu Yu in the first tea book ever written advises adding a pinch of salt when infusing the leaf. Try this at home by stewing strong, black tea, then add just add a few grains or the tea will taste

152

salty!

Sip the tea and slurp it in the mouth and note the thickness of the liquor, mouthfeel does it thicken up the saliva or have a drying effect of astringency. Note the first impression, usually floral, bitter, acid, acrid, sour, tangy, sweet. Flavours are notoriously difficult to explain to someone but dig a little deeper into the flavour profile where greens have predominantly descriptors such as grass, green, hay, butter, cream, umami, meaty. Whites and Oolongs predominate with floral, flowery, jasmine, violet, geranium, fruit, apple, citrous. Heat treatment in wok or oven roasting gives nut, hazel, almond, roast, burnt, biscuit to green tea and in black teas robust, wood, malt chocolate, caramelized, fatty, earth. When you have a general impression of the tea does the flavour last on the tongue, usually an indicator of a good tea.

The above taste adjectives is not exhaustive but an indicator of the types of flavours expected in tea. The cocktail of flavour chemicals leads to an extraordinary range of flavours and good teas have long lasting flavour.

Ditch the teabag, be adventurous and try some good quality leaf teas and finally drink it with love:-

Image by hoyas from Pixabay

CHAPTER TWELVE

RECOMMENDED SUPPLIERS

There are many suppliers of good quality teas but it is sometimes difficult to find the reliable ones soincluded are some suppliers of tea intended as a start point being reputable companies and worth a browse of their catalogues. Apologies to those I have not included but this book is about enjoying tea and not an advertising medium. No commercial gain has been requested for these recommendations in order to retain independence. Purchase good tea and do not skimp on cost and quantity in the cup.

Mei Leaf (UK)   Website: meileaf.com

This UK company is a very reliable source for some of the finest Chinese teas which Don Mei and his team personally source based on value for quality. Their online videos are an excellent source of tea information and all the teas are well described with ample information and **'SCOPE**d' - **S**eason, **C**ultivar, **O**rigin, **P**roduction, **E**levation.

Do not expect the full catalogue of teas all the time, that is not their aim, but do expect an excellent range of well chosen, ***pinnacle*** quality teas at reasonable prices. For those who want to try the teas a visit to their shop in Campden, London is well worth a visit where you can sample tea in the Chinese gong fu style they call 'True Tea' or choose to try them in the familiar European style.

Tea Box (India)   Website: www.teabox.com/

Sells a wonderful range of single estate Indian tea with the middle man cut out so the tea comes direct from source in an astonishingly short time and guaranteed to be authentic. An extremely reliable and professional company with fast delivery times and online help for any queries you may have. If you want authentic Indian single estate tea this is one place to go to.

Vadham Teas (India): www.vahdamteas.com

A competitor for Teabox selling excellent Indian teas direct with the same comments as Teabox and 100% reliable. Their Darjeeling White Tea has changed my approach to Indian white tea as it was excellent. Their tea samplers are great value and allow you to try many different teas on a theme for a reasonable price. The founder has a good ethical approach to business.

Hibiki (Japan):   www.hibiki-an.com

Japanese Green Tea of the best quality. "Hibiki" in Japanese means "touching someone's heart." Try the gyokuro, shincha or matcha for a real Japanese tea experience. Do not expect knock down prices but you do get what you pay for which is authentic, high end, good quality teas.

The Tea Makers of London (UK)   Website: www.theteamakers.co.uk/

Excellent range of mid-priced teas from around the world with customer service and superfast delivery to match and has regular promotional sales where it is worth stocking up the cupboard. 50gm packs are recommended so many different teas can be tried without overloading the tea stash cupboard. It is worth buying the tea in their containers as they are very good and it builds an easy storage of fine teas. Their Jasmine Pearls changed my views on this super fragrant tea, one of the best Jasmine teas you will find at a reasonable price.

Imperial Teas (UK):   www.imperialteas.co.uk/

Well sourced teas of all styles with excellent information about the teas, some of them quite rare. Small samples can be bought so it is a great site for trying multiple teas within your budget. Worth popping into their shop in Lincoln on aptly named Steep Hill.

Nothing But Tea: https://nbtea.co.uk/

Family run business with a selection of most teas at reasonable prices in stock with reliable quality. A good site to purchase teas to experience a selection of flavours from. This is a UK company with a passion for tea which also holds tea experience sessions advertised on their website so for a gong fu experience it looks a place to go if you are near Bedford.

Yunnan Sourcing (China)   Website:.yunnansourcing.com/

Teas direct from Yunnan from a reputable supplier. Being a Yunnan based company there is an impressive range of Puerh teas and there is a tea club where you can purchase samples either as a one-off or monthly with a discount, this being a great way to try many different teas for a reasonable price. The teas are also reassuringly pesticide tested and conform to EU standards. The shipping costs need to be taken into account but so must the tea quality and note that other sites offering free shipping have the shipping factored into the purchase price - so you pay your money and take your choice!

Moylor   https://www.moylor.com/

Teas from China. There is a wonderful selection of Puerh teas at reasonable prices and some of the more expensive puerhs can be bought as a sample making a selection of puerhs kind to the pocket. Shipping takes between 3 and 6 weeks from China.

REFERENCES

(1) All About tea, William H. Ukers, ISBN 9781365543128. The Tea and Coffee Trade Journal Company 1935

(2) Ahmed, Selena & Stepp, John. (2012). Pu-erh Tea: Botany, Production, and Chemistry. 10.13140/2.1.3619.8082.

(3) Bendall Derek S., 2011, A historical view of tea. Concourse, souvenir of World Tea Science Congress, Tocklai Experimental Station, Tea Research Association, Jorhat, pp: 3-23

(4) Meegahakumbura, Muditha & Wambulwa, Moses & Miao-miao, Li & Thapa, Kishore & Sun, Yongshuai & Moeller, Michael & Xu, Jianchu & Bo Yang, Jun & Liu, Jie & Ying Liu, Ben & Li, De-Zhu & Gao, Lian-Ming. (2018). Domestication Origin and Breeding History of the Tea Plant (Camellia sinensis) in China and India Based on Nuclear Microsatellites and cpDNA Sequence Data. Frontiers in Plant Science. 8. 10.3389/fpls.2017.02270

(5) Shinichi Nakamura Professor Kanazawa University. Introduction of KAKENHI Projects. Archeobotanical Study ofNeolithic Sites in China Sheds Light on the Origins of Lacquer and Tea Use.

(6) Ghai RR, Fuge`re V, Chapman CA, Goldberg TL, Davies TJ. 2015 Sickness behaviour associated with non-lethal infections in wild primates. Proc. R. Soc. B 282: 20151436

(7) Virginia Lovelace, Three Basic Teas and How to Enjoy them pp30 VU Books 2017 ISBN 1544112769

(8) Virginia Lovelace, Three Basic Teas and How to Enjoy them pp17 VU Books 2017 ISBN 1544112769

(9) War, Abdul R & Gabriel Paulraj, Michael & Ahad Buhroo, Abdul & Ahmad, Tariq & Hussain, Barkat & Ignacimuthu, Savarimuthu & Chand Sharma, Hari. (2012). Mechanisms of Plant Defense against Insect Herbivores. Plant signaling & behavior. 7. 10.4161/psb.21663.

(10)   Burian et al., 2016, Patterns of Stem Cell Divisions Contribute to Plant Longevity. Current Biology 26, 1385–1394, June 6, 2016

(11)Food Science and Human Wellness,ISSN: 2213-4530,Vol: 4,Issue: 1,Page: 9-27: Publication Year:2015: Tea aroma formation: Chi-Tang Hoa,, Xin Zheng , Shiming L

(12)   Peri A Tobias, David Ian Guest. Tree immunity: growing old without antibodies.Published 2014 in Trends in plant science • DOI: 10.1016/j.tplants.2014.01.011

(13)   Smilanich, Angela & Malia Fincher, R & Dyer, Lee. (2016). Does plant apparency matter? Thirty years of data provide limited support but reveal clear patterns of the effects of plant chemistry on herbivores. The New phytologist. 210. 10.1111/nph.13875

(14)   Chittka L, Peng F. Caffeine boosts bees'memories. Science. 2013;339: 1157-1159

(15)   Patent: US20100331349A1 United States

(16)   Meegahakumbura MK, Wambulwa MC, Thapa KK, Li MM, Möller M, Xu JC, et al. (2016) Indications for Three Independent Domestication Events for the Tea Plant (Camellia sinensis (L.) O. Kuntze) and New Insights into the Origin of Tea Germplasm in China and India Revealed by Nuclear Microsatellites. PLoS ONE 11(5): e0155369.

(17)   Fulian Yu and Liang Chen. Indigenous ild Tea Camellia in China. Tea Research Institute, Chinese Acadamy of Sciences

(18)   Chaturvedula, Venkata & Prakash, Indra. (2013). Tea-Aroma, Taste, Color and Bioactive Constituents. Journal of medicinal plant research. 5. 2110

(19)   War, A. R., Paulraj, M. G., Ahmad, T., Buhroo, A. A., Hussain, B., Ignacimuthu, S., & Sharma, H. C. (2012). Mechanisms of plant defense against insect herbivores. Plant signaling & behavior, 7(10), 1306-20

(20)   Bhagwat, Seema & Beecher, Gary & B Haytowitz, D & M Holden, J & Dwyer, Johanna & Peterson, Julia & E Gebhardt, S & L Eldridge, A & Agarwal, S & A Balentine, D. (2019). Flavonoid composition of tea: Comparison of black and green teas.

(21)   New discovery at the Tianluoshan site, Yuyao, Zhejiang province in 2012. From： Chinese Archaeology Date： 2013-04-17

(22)   Raj Juneja, Lekh & Chu, Djong-Chi & Tsutomu Okubo, T & Nagato, Yukiko & Yokogoshi, Hidehiko. (1999). L-theanine – a unique AmIno acid of green tea and its relaxation effect In humans. Trends in Food Science & Technology. 10. 199-204. 10.1016/S0924-2244(99)00044-8.

(23)   The Tale of Tea: A Comprehensive History of Tea from Prehistoric Times to the Present Day. George L. van Driem

42905361R00090

Printed in Poland
by Amazon Fulfillment
Poland Sp. z o.o., Wrocław